To the End,
They Remain

Raymard Clark.

To the End, They Remain

THOUGHTS ON WAR, PEACE AND RECONCILIATION

RAYMOND CLARK

For the Fallen by Lawrence Binyon (1869–1943)

...They mingle not with their laughing comrades again;
They sit no more at familiar tables at home;
They have no lot in our labour of the day-time;
They sleep beyond England's foam.
But where our desires are and our hopes profound,
Felt as a well-spring that is hidden from sight,
To the innermost heart of their own land they
are known
As the stars are known to the Night;
As the stars that shall be bright when we are dust,
Moving in marches upon the heavenly plain;
As the stars that are starry in the time of our darkness,
To the end, to the end, they remain.

First published 2013

The History Press
The Mill, Brimscombe Port
Stroud, Gloucestershire, GL5 2QG
www.thehistorypress.co.uk

© Raymond Clark, 2013

The right of Raymond Clark to be identified as the Author
of this work has been asserted in accordance with the
Copyright, Designs and Patents Act 1988.

British Library Cataloguing in Publication Data.
A catalogue record for this book is available from the British Library.

ISBN 978 0 7524 9967 3

Typesetting and origination by The History Press
Printed in Great Britain

CONTENTS

Dedication

This book is, of course, dedicated to all of our servicemen and women – past, present and future.

We must recognise that these service personnel are answerable to society for their actions whilst carrying out their duties. It is not an easy task. Whether they faced or face the Real IRA, the PLO, the INLA, the UDA or the Taliban, our men and women on the front lines were and are under the eyes of the world: the enemy often abides by no conventions. Whether the innocent suffer along the way is irrelevant, as long as they achieve their aim. In the heat of the moment, when our forces see a friend killed or maimed, is when we pray that their sense of duty will prevail.

We must also encourage all politicians, irrespective of party, to ensure that our personnel, when they return from duty or when they are discharged, receive the correct guidance. All parties promise this when they are out of power but forget their promises when in power and cuts are being asked for. Our obligation to them lies not just in a newspaper headline and a story that lasts for a few days, but it is for a lifetime. We, as individuals and as a nation, owe it to them.

Voices, from the past, the present and for the future

BATES, 'Paddy'	Major, Royal Fusiliers
BENN, Tony	Former member of Parliament
BRACKNELL, Steve	Council Member, Royal Wootton Bassett
CAMPBELL, Charles	Captain, Royal Regt of Fusiliers
CAREY, George	Former Archbishop of Canterbury
CHANTRY, June	Lyricist
CHILDREN OF NI	Bethany Brown
	Alex King
	Olivia Novaes
	Christopher Wilson
CLARK Allen	MI Intelligence Officer and veterans' champion
CLARK, Raymond	Ex soldier and author
CLEGG, Simon	Chief Executive of Ipswich Town FC
COCKSWORTH, Christopher	Bishop of Coventry
COWLEY, Nigel	GP, Bournemouth
DALEY, Cahal	Cardinal of All Ireland and Bishop of Armagh
DANNATT, Francis	GOC NI
DOBBS, Michael	Former MP, author
DODD, Ken	Singer, comedian
DONALDSON, Jeffrey	MP and MLA, Lisburn, NI
ELLIOT, John	Former editor of *Soldier* magazine
ESSEX, David	Actor and singer
FELLOWES, Julian	Author, actor
FINNEGAN, Terry	Colonel, NATO, NORAD
FINNEY, Christopher	Lance Corporal, Blues and Royals
GAUNT, Francis	Sergeant, Irish Guards
GREEN, Liz	Mother of soldier killed, NI
GREEN, Val (Clark)	Aunt of soldier killed in NI

GUTHRIE, Charles	Former Chief of Defence staff
HALL, James	Former Lieutenant (RA), author
HAIN, Peter	Former Secretary of State
HART DYKE, David	Former Officer RN, Falklands War
HAYMAN, Helene	Former Speaker House of Lords, Baroness
HEAD, Christopher	Captain Royal Regt of Fusiliers
HILL, William 'Billy'	Corporal Royal Regt of Fusiliers
HORNUNG, Otter	Refugee, Colonel
HUGHES, Kim	Warrant Officer
HOLDEN, Amanda	Actress, TV personality
JAMES, Margot	Conservative Party Vice Chairman
JACKSON, 'Mike'	Chief of Staff
KELLY, Matthew	Presenter, actor
LUMLEY, Joanna	Actress, presenter, activist
LYNN, Vera	Singer
MAGEE, Muriel	Mother, poet, NI
MARR, Simon	Commanding Officer, Royal Regt Fusiliers
McCONNELL, Jack	Former First Minister, Scotland
McKENNA, Virginia	Actress, conservationist
MORGAN, Hywel	Former First Minister for Wales
MORRIS, Raymond	Laird of Balgorrie
MOUNTBATTEN, Patricia	Countess Mountbatten of Burma
MULHERN RSM	WO1 Royal Regt Fusiliers
NORTHUMBERLAND	Duke
NORTON, Peter	Captain, VC
OSGOOD, Alan	A child during war
OSGOOD, Judith (nee Hall)	A child evacuee
PAISLEY, Ian	Reverend, former MP
PARRY, Colin	Father of Tim, killed in Warrington Bomb
P (ANONYMOUS)	A product of a divided Ireland/Island
PEACE PROTESTORS, London	Dawn Evans and a friend

PRIESTS, The	Singing Roman Catholic Priests. NI
	Fr Delargy
	Fr E. O'Hagan
	Fr O. O'Hagan
PUTTNAM, David	Film director
REES, Tim	Ex Welsh Guard
REID, John	Former Home Secretary
RIDLEY, Matthew	Viscount, 2Lt Coldstream Guards
RIPPON, Angela	Presenter
SISTERS REMEMBER	Monica Dawson (née Clark)
	Elizabeth Dalton (née Clark)
SPEAKMAN, William	VC winner, Korea
TEBBITT, Norman	Cabinet Minister
THEOBALD, Peter and Frances	Founders of 'Living Memorials'
TURNER, John	Soldier, RA
WATT, Charles 'Reddy'	General, president of Combat Stress
WELLWOOD, Thomas	Teenage war worker, Sunderland
WHARTON, Ken	Former soldier, author
WIDDECOMBE, Ann	Former MP
WILLIAMS, Shirley	Baroness
WILLS, David	Retired Brigadier, President of Royal British Legion

About this book

A few years ago, Ray Clark had a simple idea: send postcards to those who might share their thoughts with others on loss, remembrance, war and peace. The response was remarkable. Men and women from all walks of life, from the Cabinet, the House of Lords and the senior ranks of the British Army to ex-servicemen, journalists and war widows, felt moved to express their feelings in a few words on those postcards. Some are simple reminiscences; some are more profound. This book will sadden, provoke and inspire.

All the royalties on sales will go to two charities. The first is Help for Heroes, established in 2007 working for the wounded of the British Armed forces, an astonishingly successful organisation responsible for huge capital projects like the £8.5m Rehabilitation Complex at Headley Court, as well as providing funds to wounded individual members of the armed forces according to need. The second is Action Cancer, providing early detection, counselling and support services and cancer prevention education. They were there for Ray when his wife was diagnosed as terminally ill. This book has been created with love and gratitude.

INTRODUCTION
BY RAYMOND CLARK

At the end of the First World War, when the American president Woodrow Wilson spoke of 'the war to end all wars', did the world actually believe it? After the loss of millions upon millions of men, women and children of all nationalities and creeds across the globe, did the world really think it would never happen again? Since then, there have been many more wars and conflicts resulting in poverty, injuries and, of course, many more deaths.

This book will allow you to share the thoughts, the pain, the anguish, the tears and the hopes for the future not only of those who have been involved but also of those who may become involved in the years ahead.

To achieve this I had a series of postcards with military themes sponsored for charity, and these were sent out to the famous and the not so famous. People were asked if they could write a few words on the reverse of the card expressing their thoughts and feelings about conflict. Many people obliged and their thoughts were touching and meaningful. Some felt that they could not justify their thoughts in a few lines and wrote letters. These are also included.

I hope that this book will encourage you to realise that the victims of greed and power are not just those who are maimed and killed. Victims are also those who are left behind and even those not yet born. These are the thoughts of fathers, mothers, wives, sisters, brothers, sons and daughters and of peace protestors. The book's aim is to show that everyone is affected in their own way.

Anger, bitterness, futility, hopelessness, pride, love, fellowship, tears and frustration, they are all in evidence in the following pages. But almost all appear to have one thing in common, and that is hope.

Three cards were sent out.

This one featured a Drum Head Service. Such a service was often held throughout history in the field, when no altar or table was available; the regimental drums were used, draped, if available, with the Colours of the regiment. The photograph was taken at a Remembrance Sunday service at the Moravian Church in Lower Ballinderry, just outside of Lisburn in Northern Ireland. (Photograph by kind permission of Mr Roy Brown)

HEROES - PAST AND PRESENT

This featured servicemen past and present: members of the Household Cavalry in London; Sergeant Richardson of the Labour Corps in the First World War and a citation from the Labour Corps; and the late Sgt Bruce Hodgson, Royal Northumberland Fusiliers (Aden/BAOR/GB/Northern Ireland).

'SOLDIERS OF THE QUEEN'

This one shows various regiments on public duties in London: at St James's Palace, Horse Guards Parade and the Tower of London.

British Service Personnel Killed in Conflicts Since 1945

This list has been compiled from various sources and is open to interpretation. If there have been fatalities other than those listed at the time of writing, then I sincerely apologise.

Northern Ireland	1,298*
Malaya	340
Falkland Islands	255
Palestine	233
Cyprus	105
Aden	68
Egypt	54
Balkans	48
Gulf	47**
Yangtse	46
Oman	24
Suez	22
Borneo	16
Kenya	12
Sierra Leone	1
Korea	765
Afghanistan	444***
Iraq	176

*   This figure includes not only those service personnel who died or were killed in Northern Ireland but also those who were killed on mainland Britain and in Europe because of 'the Troubles'. Each individual is named on a 'Roll of Honour' as listed by The Northern Ireland Veterans Association.

**   This figure includes nine personnel killed by 'friendly fire'.

*** This figure is correct at time of going to press.

British Involvement in Conflicts Since the Second World War

1944–1947	Greek Civil War
1945–1948	Indo China
1945–1946	Austria
1945–1948	India
1945–1948	Palestine
1945–1960	Malaya
1948	Berlin Airlift
1947–1991	The Cold War*
1950–1953	Korea
1951–1954	Suez Canal
1952–1960	Kenya
1955–1959 and 1987	Cyprus
1963–1967	Aden
1956	Suez
1957	Muscat and Oman
1958	Jordan
1962–1966	Borneo
1964	Ugandan Army Mutiny
1969–1976	Oman and Dhofar
1969–	Northern Ireland
1982	Falkland Islands
1990-1991	Gulf War
1992-1995	Bosnia
1998-1999	Kosovo
2000	Sierra Leone
2001–	Afghanistan
2003–2011	Iraq
2010	Libya

* The dates of the beginning and end of the Cold War are difficult to define. Did the Cold War actually end with the fall of the Berlin Wall? Is it really over? The same question is asked by some of the Iraq War. Troops were often deployed well before the official start of hostilities, so some of these dates are a little misleading.

British Service Personnel have also been represented in the deployment of agencies such as the UN and NATO in the following locations:

Bermuda	Antigua
Pakistan	Egypt
Lebanon	Rhodesia
New Hebrides	Kurdistan
Yemen	Angola
Rwanda	Congo
East Timor	Macedonia

Almost 250 years ago, Edmund Burke warned the Commons against repressing the American 'rebellion': 'The use of force alone is but temporary. It may subdue for a moment but it does not remove the necessity of subduing again; and a nation is not governed which is perpetually to be conquered ... An armament is not a victory.' Looking at these lists brings these words to mind. Perhaps they should be at the forefront of the thinking of politicians when they formulate foreign policy.

FOREWORD
BY KEN WHARTON

Raymond Clark has put together an excellent book about war, peace and reconciliation. The words within are not peacenik bleatings; they tell an impassioned story about the role of the most unsung hero of British – or, indeed, any – modern society: the soldier.

It is worth noting that in the sixty-eight years of 'peace' – as I write – since the end of the Second World War, there has only been one year in which a British soldier has not died on active service; that year was 1968, the year before Northern Ireland became collectively insane. The author and contributors speak of 'normal' families and also speak of heroes who gave their all in the last world war and of those who have paid the supreme sacrifice. They speak of those who made major contributions to the securing of peace and liberty and in ensuring the freedom of generations. Ray points out that the IRA made people leave Northern Ireland, either through violence or through intimidation; one wonders, had Hitler been successful and occupied Britain, just how the SS would have treated Irish reunification groups.

The book is seen through the eyes of soldiers, through evacuee children and youngsters who stayed behind to watch the 'spectacle' of modern warfare that raged in the blue skies overhead in 1940. Ray looks at many conflicts since the last world war, including Korea and the award of a VC to a soldier who was ultimately – in my opinion – destroyed by the fame and public acclaim. Of particular poignancy is war as seen through the eyes of one of 'the brides of Christ', a nun who observed the conflict under Nazi occupation.

We see war through the eyes of myriad contributors – from children to soldiers facing cavalry charges in far-off lands in far-off times. I commend this book to everyone, even those who hate war with a passion. Read Raymond's words and I guarantee that if you hate war, you will see that there is a group within our society who hates it even more than you do: the soldiers who shed their blood to defend your right to make choices.

Raymond cleverly and interestingly links conflicts from the First World War in Syria to the last world war through the bombing of Coventry and on to the struggle in the far outposts of the former Empire ending with the tragedy of Afghanistan. I am a former serving soldier who saw action on the streets of Belfast, and I am honoured not only to be allowed to write this foreword but also to be associated with this work.

Ken Wharton is the author of six books on the Northern Ireland Troubles, including *Bloody Belfast: An Oral History of the British Army's War against the IRA*; *The Bloodiest Year, 1972: British Soldiers in Northern Ireland in Their Own Words*; and *Wasted Years, Wasted Lives Volume One: The British Army in Northern Ireland 1975–77*.

THE CONTRIBUTORS:
THOUGHTS ON WAR,
PEACE AND RECONCILIATION

British Soldier in AFGHANISTAN

'We are told that we are not allowed to give any interviews to the press unless it is done via an appointed officer in your unit and then approved by the Ministry of Defence. I assume that the MOD has learnt a lot since Iraq. Although they can probably trace me from some of the following information it is as far as I wish to go and wish to remain anonymous.

'I am a 27-year-old married man on my second tour of Afghanistan and shall be leaving the forces in a few years. I think that my wife has had enough of the unknown and wants to settle down to a normal life and have a family.

'Work in Afghanistan is long, very hot and at times tedious, but not boring. Although days may appear routine they are not, there is always the unexpected. It is the unexpected that becomes normal, you are always aware and looking out for the unexpected and the abnormal. Sometimes it feels that we make one step forward, only for it to be followed by two steps backwards. If the British can not win the hearts and minds of the people no one will, certainly not our "gung ho" allies.

'I was asked whilst on leave if we would ever win. All I can say is that I honestly do not know. It is inevitable that we shall have to go the way of other conflicts and speak to the enemy, be it the IRA, the Cypriots or the Mau Mau. So why not start before more lives are lost?

'It is fantastic that we have such great support from our families and the British people; it is not fantastic that the government of the day do not instill any confidence in the troops.

'We see innocence every day, we see smiles every day, we see hope every day but we also see fear every day. Fear of the unknown. Fear of what will happen to those people who helped us once we leave. We have our pin-ups; we mark the days off our calendars, we write home and talk about the future. We phone and e-mail when the opportunity permits. We even try to

kill time by trying to get the "body-beautiful", I think for me though that's a waste of time!

'You become angry when a friend or someone from your unit is killed or injured. You are sorry for them and their families but deep inside you are unashamedly grateful that it is not you. It is being selfish but being honest.

'All I can say is that we are doing what we knew was expected of us when we enlisted. We are paid for our work. Our loved ones knew, but hope that it never happens, that we could end up as fatalities.

'I hope that the country does not get involved with Syria. The poor will always be poor, the country will only prosper if we stop giving money to governments and give it instead in the form of supplies to registered organisations with the help of the United Nations.

'The only people who benefit from internal conflicts are the makers and suppliers of weapons. The corrupt rich become richer and more powerful but the innocent will continue to suffer.'

BATES, Major Roy 'Paddy'

Former Major, the Royal (City of London Regt) Fusiliers
Fisherman
Pirate Radio Broadcaster
Founder of the 'Principality' of Sealand

[His son, 'Prince' Michael, tells this story.] 'As a young subaltern in Syria with a dozen or so men, Paddy was confronted by some native cavalry commanded by a French officer. He got his men to "dig in" and placed his two Bren guns at either end of the trench. The Bren had quite a slow rate of fire compared to modern weapons and a relatively small magazine to hold the ammo. These were backed up by the other infantrymen's standard issue, similarly slow-firing bolt action .303-calibre Lee Enfield rifles.

'The French officer gave the command, and the cavalry charged across the plain towards them. As they came closer and closer with a thundering of hooves, my father clambered out of the trench and held up his arms for them to stop, pointing to the Bren guns on either side. The charging mass feinted, turned and galloped back to their original position without a shot being fired. My father then explained to me, as if it was yesterday, that he saw the French officer riding up and down the ranks of horsemen slapping their backs with the flat of his sabre to drive them on for another go.

'Once again, they thundered across the plain intent on impaling my old man and his comrades on their lances. Once again, he climbed from the trenches and pointed at the guns with the probably misplaced confidence of a young Englishman in a foreign land. Yet again, the lancers feinted and retired; this time they kept going and left the field of combat. I was astounded when he told me this story as a young man.

"Why did you not just stay in the comparative safety of the trench and mow them down? Surely you felt threatened by all the tons of horseflesh and steel charging at you with deadly intent? Why did you put yourself at risk? Why did you do it?" His understated answer was, one would like to be able to claim, singularly British.

"I thought I had the situation in hand, but more importantly, I didn't want to kill the horses."

'It must have been the last cavalry charge of the Second World War, and there must be a few men alive today who can be thankful we come from a nation of animal lovers. Paddy ended the war as a major in The 1st Btn the Royal Fusiliers, City of London Regiment.'

BENN, Anthony ('Tony') Neil Wedgwood

1943	*RAF Pilot in South Africa and Rhodesia*
1964–1966	*Post Master General*
1963–1983	*MP for Bristol*
1984–2001	*MP for Chesterfield*

Tony Benn is a retired British Labour Party politician who was an MP for fifty years and a Cabinet minister under Harold Wilson and James Callaghan. He has been the president of the Stop the War coalition for more than a decade. What is claimed to be the largest demonstration in British history was organised by the coalition on 15 February 2003, against the invasion of Iraq. Tony Benn was a key speaker at the event.

> "Jaw Jaw is better than War War"
> Winston Churchill
>
> I agree.

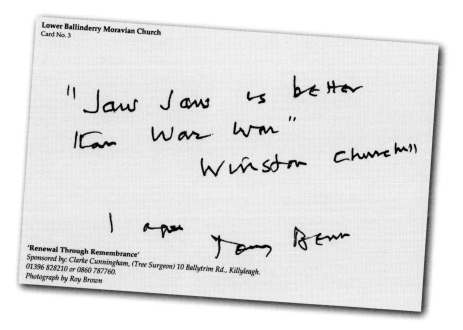

Lower Ballinderry Moravian Church
Card No. 3

'Renewal Through Remembrance'
Sponsored by: Clarke Cunningham, (Tree Surgeon) 10 Ballytrim Rd., Killyleagh.
01396 828210 or 0860 787760.
Photograph by Roy Brown

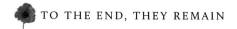
BRACKNELL, Steve

Wootton Bassett Council

The people of Wootton Bassett took it upon themselves to show our fallen young heroes and heroines the respect that was due and owed to them on their repatriation. The town came to a standstill. The Standards of The Royal British Legion were unfurled and dipped as the cortege passed by. As the fatalities grew, so did the media coverage. The number of people lining the street to pay their respects increased. Relatives, loved ones, friends, school friends, ex-service personnel and many, many more attended the homecomings. The town was granted the title of 'Royal Wootton Bassett' in 2011 by Her Majesty the Queen. The honour was presented by HRH Princess Anne, the Princess Royal, on behalf of the Queen. The ceremony was attended by leading politicians including PM David Carmeron.

> 'With very best wishes from the Mayor of Wootton Bassett. Thank you for your letter and your support. War is not inevitable, but neither is Peace. The only way we can repay the sacrifice of the fallen, is to remember them.'

CAMPBELL, Charles Ashley Oliver

Captain, 1st Btn The Royal Regiment of Fusiliers
Awarded the Military Cross whilst serving in Iraq as a Lieutenant.

> 'It is a rare privilege to command men
> who are capable of turning their hand
> from high intensity conflict to securing
> peace, and through so doing, are
> prepared to make the ultimate sacrifice.'

Lower Ballinderry Moravian Church
Card No. 3

It is a rare privilege to command men who are capable of turning their hand from high intensity conflict to securing peace, and through so doing are prepared to make the ultimate sacrifice.

CAPT C O CAMPBELL MC 1RRF

'Renewal Through Remembrance'
Sponsored by: Clarke Cunningham, (Tree Surgeon) 10 Ballytrim Rd., Killyleagh.
01396 828210 or 0860 787760.
Photograph by Roy Brown

CAREY, George Leonard, 103rd Archbishop of Canterbury

Archbishop of Canterbury 1991–2002
Created a life peer in 2002 as Baron Carey of Clifton in the City and County
of Bristol

The prime minister, Margaret Thatcher, put his name forward to the Queen for appointment as Archbishop of Canterbury. *The Times* newspaper commented: 'Mrs Thatcher's known impatience with theological and moral wooliness … will have been a factor.'

> 'Such is the awfulness of War, I have often
> echoed the words of Benjamin Franklin:
> "There never was a good war or a bad peace".'

CHANTRY, June

At a Remembrance Service at the Great Barlow Branch (Cheshire) of The Royal British Legion, new words to an old tune were sung. The words were written by June Chantry. They are poignant and very meaningful, and for that reason, with her kind permission, I include them here for you to ponder.

Hymn for Those at War
Tune: Eventide: 'Abide with Me'

We ask you, Lord, for countries torn by strife:
shells, and starvation, threatening every life.
In their distress and need, still let them hear,
"See, I am with you; trust and do not fear."

Guard those who fight, and comfort those who mourn.
Stay with the orphans, helpless and forlorn.
Reveal to them your love, and let them hear.
"I will be with you; trust and do not fear."

Bless those who come to bring relief and aid;
driven by love, though many feel afraid.
On every journey, let them wait to hear.
"I'm ever with you; trust and do not fear."

Give guidance to the seekers after peace;
bless their endeavours, let the firing cease.
Yet, while it lasts, still grant that they may hear,
"You are my children; trust and do not fear."

Grant that some good may soften every crime,
though wars continue to the end of time;
and may we pray that all in need shall hear:
"God be with you; trust and do not fear."

CHILDREN OF NORTHERN IRELAND:
BROWN, Bethany
KING, Alex
NOVAES, Olivia
WILSON, Christopher

Lower Ballinderry Primary School, Lisburn, Northern Ireland
Headmaster – Mr Thompson

At my request, Mr Thompson asked the children what they thought and felt about peace.

Bethany Brown, a pupil at the school, had told her teacher about a visit to her Granny who lives near the 'Peace Wall' in Belfast. This wall was erected to 'protect' the residents of both communities from one another. One day whilst visiting her Granny, she saw a small bird trapped in a crack in the wall, and in her mind that small bird became a symbol of peace. Bethany sat down with several of her friends, and the following poem and picture is the result of their combined thoughts.

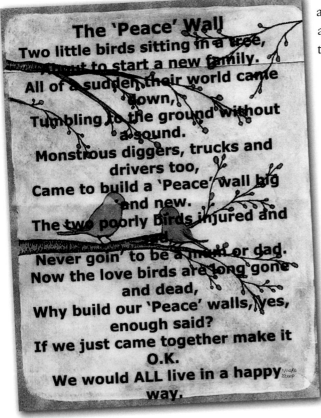

The 'Peace' Wall
Two little birds sitting in a tree,
____ to start a new family.
All of a sudden their world came
down,
Tumbling to the ground without
a sound.
Monstrous diggers, trucks and
drivers too,
Came to build a 'Peace' wall big
and new.
The two poorly birds injured and
___,
Never goin' to be a mum or dad.
Now the love birds are long gone
and dead,
Why build our 'Peace' walls, yes,
enough said?
If we just came together make it
O.K.
We would ALL live in a happy
way.

Another pupil, Christopher Wilson, decided to create his own view of the Peace Wall and put two birds in his drawing; these birds were looking at the nest they had built in a tree adjacent to the building of the actual wall and talking about their future:

First bird, 'I was going to be a Dad.'
Second bird, 'And I was going to be a Mum, now what will happen?'

Note the differences in the child's view of the wall and the reality.

Clark, Allen B., Jnr

Two years after graduation from West Point, Allen Clark volunteered for a tour in Vietnam, where he served as a Military Intelligence Officer assigned to the Fifth Special Forces Group. He sustained injuries in an early morning mortar attack on June 17, 1967, that necessitated the amputation of both legs below his knees. His military service and sacrifice were recognized with the receipt of a Silver Star for Gallantry in Action, the Purple Heart, and the Combat Infantryman's Badge. In 1989, he became assistant secretary for Veterans' Liaison and Program Coordination at the US Department of Veterans Affairs. He is the author of *Wounded Soldier, Healing Warrior* and *Valor in Vietnam 1963–1977: Chronicles of Honor, Courage, and Sacrifice.*

'As I arose shortly before 4 a.m. on June 17, 1967 there was no hint that this day would change my life forever. I went inside the inner perimeter at Dak To Special Forces Camp in the Central Highlands of Vietnam to pull my two hour alert duty shift until dawn. It would be six hours before my commanding officer would arrive from 280 miles away in Saigon to remove me from Dak To because the enemy noose was tightening. In the previous week two patrols had been ambushed just miles from our camp and four of five Americans were killed. A hardcore battalion of North Vietnamese Army regulars had infiltrated from the Ho Chi Minh Trail in Laos.

'My mission as a Military Intelligence officer assigned to the Army's Green Berets under an assumed name with the mission to recruit native Montagnards to gather intelligence on the enemy in neighboring Cambodia was threatened due to the heavy enemy activity in the nearby jungles. However, we had a modest sense of security that morning because the U.S. Army's 173rd Airborne Brigade was to begin arriving to fight the North Vietnamese Army troops pouring into our area.

'Between 4 a.m. and half past I was between two worlds, one had been relatively peaceful because for the previous twenty-five years it was defined as almost idyllic. Raised in a patriotic army family with two wonderful loving parents, I had accepted Jesus Christ as my Savior as a teenager. My dream of being a cadet at West Point from which I had graduated in 1963 had been fulfilled. Soon after graduation I had married after a short courtship. My tour in the war zone was almost up. After one more year on active duty in Maryland I would begin the good life in Dallas, Texas, having submitted my resignation. We all live between two worlds; one of Caesar's and one of God's. In Caesar's world I was a confident dedicated Army Captain with an attitude. In God's world admittedly I was not so confident. However, the ensuing turmoil and conflict about to enter my life would propel me to strengthen my faith to attain a semblance of peace.

'At 4:30 a.m. the enemy, having moved at a rapid pace from the ambush sites, began a heavy mortar barrage into the inner perimeter where I sat quietly in the camp dining room writing a letter to my wife. Immediately I went outside, stood in the open, began to attempt to pinpoint the enemy firing positions, arrange counter-battery fire and place flares into the dark night when I was thrust forward on my stomach with a harsh, crushing blow caused I later learned from a mortar round landing eighteen inches to my left rear, traumatically removing my left leg below the knee. My right leg was amputated ten days later. My world was turned upside down. Then I began a multi-year struggle to recover from the bloody aftermath of the horrific wounding compounded by the spiritual warfare induced by severe Post-Traumatic Stress Disorder.

'A fifteen-month hospitalization allowed me to walk on artificial legs. However, during my hospitalization, fears for my future began to overtake me and I was admitted to a closed psychiatric ward for fourteen weeks of the most agonizing challenge in my life. It was a time of heavy dosages of anti-depressants which lasted with psychotherapy until 1973. At that time I began, by the grace of my Savior, to begin what I have called the beginning of acceptance of the Lordship of God. I began to understand the extraordinary power of prayer, the ultimate eternal struggle and conflict of mankind between God and the devil, and at my own level the spiritual warfare we face individually. As a soldier I was trained to face conflict on a strategic level, but had no inkling of the tactical conflict I would face on the personal level.

'Maturation of my faith and my knowledge has brought me to a point of understanding that, individually as military people and especially as people in violent conditions, we face conflict, bloodshed, and pain because, from the beginning of recorded history, the ruling kings, potentates, dictators, tribal leaders, and even in modern times elected leaders, have sought to use their power to reflect their greed and selfish motives to yoke their own people and impose their will on others most often by violent means. Sadly, I am convinced that this pattern of world history will not end until, in the view of my Christian faith, my Savior returns and the Millennial Kingdom begins.

'It was in the mid-1970s that I believe I was grafted into the scarlet thread that is ours as Christians when we truly believe with faith that Jesus died on the cross for our sins. This new change of my heart was the only path for me to achieve personal peace. New conflicts have interrupted my peace all my life, but I was now armed in a new way to seek and achieve personal peace. During those years of healing it was not easy to be my wife and my marriage eventually ended in divorce after thirty years. It was a struggle not to be angry, sad and lacking in self-confidence. Business endeavors led to personal and corporate bankruptcy, not due to mismanagement, but due to tax law changes and market conditions. At age 52 I found myself one night with a bank balance of under $10. Both parents died of horrific cancer at age 68. I have survived multiple medical challenges to include prostate cancer, a kidney disease, constant skin breakdowns, and a fall which broke my femur. But, I never gave up. I recall vividly the words of Winston Churchill, "Never never never give in."

'My own experiences with healing motivated me to begin my lay ministry, Combat Faith, www.combatfaith.com), which has a major section to help my fellow veterans heal from their combat operating stressors from our wars.

'God is not finished with me yet, but He has taken me a long distance from that scared young captain in the hospital wards in San Antonio 1967–68. I praise and thank Him each day. In 2004 I remarried the former Linda Frost with whom I jointly minister when she does dramatic presentations of Women of the Bible. Together with my new life with her and my Lord I have achieved a personal peace.'

CLARK, Raymond BEM

Former Band SNCO
Royal Northumberland Fusiliers
St George's Band, The Royal Regiment of Fusiliers
Author, part-time retail worker
Charity Volunteer
Awarded the British Empire Medal in 2013 for charity works

'As a young lad growing up in the North East of England we were of a generation that played "Cowboys and Indians", "Japs and Americans" and "English and Germans". We watched war films on black and white TV if you had one, or at the matinees at the local "flea pit" on a Saturday afternoon and then re-enacted the whole thing on the way home. We were immune to the deaths as it was just a case of the "baddies against the goodies".

'I never thought that one day I would join the army, in fact having two older brothers, it was considered, especially by my PE teacher at school, that I was not the one who would join up; but join up I did.

'I remember the young Corporal from the recruitment office in Newcastle coming out to our terraced house and speaking to me and Dad about the options. I said that I would like to be a cook and he explained what it all involved but as soon as he mentioned "guns" I did not want that. He asked if I played any musical instrument and when I said yes he immediately replied "Then why not join the Band. They never touch weapons, nor guard duties." So off to the Band I went. (I wish now that I could take him to court for giving me the incorrect information!)

'What a shattering experience, all that physical exercise (no hand written excuse-me notes here), running against a man built like the proverbial, with a funny-shaped ball in his hand, climbing ropes – what had I done?

'At that time in 1963, we "band boys", as we were affectionately known, did not have weapons and did no weapon training; then in 1966, the Regiment, The Royal Northumberland Fusiliers, were to be sent on a nine-month unaccompanied tour of duty in Aden. At that time Aden was hitting the news because of unrest as the people agitated for independence. Soldiers and civilians were being attacked. We were sent to Waterloo Lines, a camp just outside of RAK Kormaska. One of the Regiment's duties was to look after the town of Crater, built in the actual crater of a volcano. It was a town comprising a warren of streets and many, many cars, in fact it was the most 'car-populated' town in the world. Yes, you have probably

guessed – the Band were issued with weapons and carried out guard duties, bus escorts (escorting service children to and from school and home – many were in Malla, (known as "murder mile"). To watch us mount guard and present arms was, as my father would have said, like watching "Fred Karno's Army" – chaotic, but eventually we mastered it.

'The Regiment lost nine men in June of 1967 and they were buried in Silent Valley in Aden. At that time, bodies were not automatically repatriated and if you wished a body to be brought home then you had to pay for it yourself.

'The late 1960s saw trouble break out on the streets of Belfast and Londonderry (Derry), which spread to other towns and villages, between the Protestant and Catholic Communities. This immediately created a conundrum about the deployment of soldiers in the British Army from Northern Ireland and what effect it would have on them. For a short while, those soldiers were not allowed to serve and normally remained on duties in England. The Regiment went several times and we as a Band often either accompanied them or visited them to entertain or carry out PR work in the community. We played at a local community hall in Londonderry once and one of the pieces we played was currently in the charts, sung by Lee Marvin, called "I was born under a Wanderin' Star". As we played it some of the audience broke into song but changed the lyrics to "I was born under a Union Jack". Needless to say, it was taken off future programmes. We even managed to keep the slightly chaotic reputation of the Band alive within the Regiment when we were on guard duties at a housing estate just outside of Ebrington Barracks, which housed both service and civilian families. One of the bandsmen managed to set fire to the sangar. When asked why he had not quickly communicated this unfortunate incident by telephone line he replied, "Because that's on fire too."

'When the Regiment went to Belfast for a six-month tour, three senior NCOs from the Band were "requested" to join with another SNCO from the Regiment. We were to work in The Royal Victoria Hospital as liaison officers. This involved interviewing anyone injured by the Troubles, be they civilians or members of the security forces. We also attended the operating theatre to collect evidence. We arranged for guards from the Regiment to be provided for anyone admitted that needed protection. We saw young men with their knee caps blown away, young men shot in the spine and paralysed, young women tarred and feathered for fraternising, and men, women and children caught up in the violence. The corridor would be covered in blood from injuries caused by bombs placed where students would drink, in betting shops on Grand National Day, in supermarkets and restaurants, injuring and killing the innocent. People were frightened of going out, of going to cinemas at night. They were frightened of other people. But they did have resilience and tried to carry on life as normal, they accepted being searched as they went into M&S and Boots …

'Once, as part of my twelve-hour shift I was informed by Casualty Reception that there was a man being treated who was waving a gun at the staff. It was my turn to go up. He was accusing the doctor and nurse of giving priority to the "Brits". After what seemed an eternity, to me at least, he handed the weapon over, which was found not to be loaded – but my churning stomach did not know that!

'In 1979 the Peace Agreement was signed and everyone thought that life would return to normal and that it would be given back to the people to enjoy, but in Northern Ireland what is "normal"? Still things remained unsettled and remain that way for the foreseeable future.

'In 1994, along with my wife and daughter, I relocated to a small village outside of Lisburn to live with my wife's father. I had met my wife, who was English, in the Royal Victoria Hospital, where she was affectionately known as "the f**g Brit" who worked on casualty reception. There were murals on both Catholic and Protestant estates, Orangemen could not walk down the Queen's Highway, kerbstones were painted either red, white and blue, or orange, green and white. Flags supporting the Israeli cause were flown in Protestant areas, flags supporting the Palestinian cause were flown in Catholic areas. As an ex-serviceman, I was once threatened with being driven out of Northern Ireland by local loyalists because I dared to auction a signed picture of the Pope to raise funds for a local charity. Later, I was stopped on the way to hospital to see my wife who was dying from cancer by loyalists at a barricade. They were trying to bring the country to a standstill.

'It will take many, many years for the mindless inherited bigotry, on both sides, to be removed from society.

'I feel strongly that we as a nation must take a stand for ourselves. We must stop being the world's policemen. We must, as some other European nations do, put ourselves first and others second and not as we currently do. Along with the USA we are branded the Satans of the world, but if that is the case then why do those who despise us want to come and live amongst us? Why do we permit it? Why can they not demonstrate and agitate in their own country? Simply because they have the right to do it here, without fear. In their own country they would lose all their rights. We must also ensure that the United Nations is not the paper tiger that it currently is, it must be able to act at the time and not have to refer back to politicians in Whitehall and Washington.

'We must ensure that the human rights of the silent majority, of the innocent, the helpless, the defenceless, are adhered to and protected, because at the current time these rights are being eroded by successive governments of all persuasions, to such an extent that in my opinion it verges on political madness. Like many people, I try to be an optimist and believe that what our politicians say they will do, they will. But it seems to me they often do what is best for them and not for the people they govern. To govern law abiding people is easy. To govern and control evil is difficult. We must all encourage hope in one another and talk with our neighbours to nurture the question in every heart: "What can I do for others?"'

CLEGG, Simon

Chief Executive of Ipswich Town Football Club

'As Hegel once said, "The only thing we learn from History is that we learn nothing from History." Too often politicians around the globe forget this and create wars and conflicts with the most terrible consequences. Global peace is a worthy goal but sadly unattainable until man learns to control his ambition.'

COCKSWORTH, The Right Reverend
Dr Christopher John, Bishop of Coventry

Christopher Cocksworth was consecrated as bishop on July 2008, the youngest serving diocesan bishop in the Church of England. He was formerly principal of Ridley Hall, Cambridge.

'I preached at a funeral of a young Fusilier in Coventry Cathedral. He had been blown up while trying to rescue his Platoon Sergeant who was also under fire in Afghanistan. At the funeral there were several other young fusiliers with bodies battered and damaged by war.

'The coffin carrying the dead, the wounded bearing such pain, the Cathedral holding so much grief brought home the awful horror of war and the urgent need to find peace.

'The only peace that will last is one based – as Coventry Cathedral, ruined by war and rebuilt by faith and hope, tells in stone – on reconciliation. Reconciliation that begins with the costly crying out to God "Father, Forgive" and reaching out to enemies with a determination to build a safer, better, more Christ-like world.

Yours in Christ

Christopher'

On 15 November 1940, in a massive raid lasting over ten hours, approximately 500 aircraft of the Luftwaffe bombed the city and left it devastated; 4,330 homes were destroyed, three-quarters of all factories were damaged and two hospitals were destroyed. Between 330 and 540 people lost their lives with many more injured and homeless. The fourteenth-century cathedral was all but destroyed. The Cathedral Provost said, 'The cathedral will rise again, will be rebuilt, and it will be a great pride to future generations as it has been to past generations.' The new cathedral was completed and dedicated on the 25 May 1963 and stands alongside the skeleton of the war-damaged ruin.

COWLEY, Dr Nigel, MB CLB MRCGP DRCOG DCH Dip Med ed

Doctor, Denmark Road Medical Centre, Dorset

'I am lucky to have been born into a generation which has not personally been touched by war. My grandfathers were affected by two world wars but my parents only remember cities being bombed in their childhood.

'We have now "enjoyed" world peace for 68 years. The conflicts in which our troops have been engaged have been remote, The Falklands, The Balkans, Iraq and Afghanistan. Furthermore our experience of these wars is, for the most of us, remote and sanitised through television. Watching a precision-guided missile hitting its target with pinpoint accuracy during the first invasion of Iraq gave me a reassuring feeling that we were now waging a war where innocent civilians would not be affected. This modern warfare does not really engage our moral mind. We are able to justify our action and to justify war with logic and reason. In particular, we do not need to encourage our emotions and allow them to question the morality of what we do and how we do it. I remember feeling so emotionally disengaged with the Falklands conflict that it almost felt like we were watching the unfolding of a cricket or football match. The national media played a major part. *The Sun* fuelled our nationalism with two classic headlines, "Stick it up your Junta" and hailed the sinking of the Belgrano and the death of 275 men with "Gotcha". Victory over Argentina in the Falklands was the closest we have come in the national psyche to victory over West Germany in 1966.

'Apart from reservations about how we decide to go to war, I am also anxious about who we send to war. Adolescents think and act very differently from the rest of the population. They are experiencing that awkward transition from complete dependency of childhood to complete independence of adulthood. Their brains are undergoing enormous changes and as yet their frontal lobes are not sufficiently developed to suppress their primal and basic desires and instincts. This maturation of the frontal part of the brain is not complete until they are in their early 20s. Until then the brain is vulnerable to psychological trauma. After that time the brain remains vulnerable but has better coping mechanisms. In other words, we do not need to send teenagers to war; we can allow them to mature and become psychologically more equipped to deal with the emotional terror of close contact.

'I have a gnawing feeling inside me that we take young impressionable men and we mould and brainwash them into efficient fighting machines. I do not know the psychological techniques that are employed to ensure that soldiers carry out their missions; inevitably this must require them to bypass their limbic system. I also do not know that the long-term psychological consequences there are for such training but it doesn't feel morally right.

'Taking all these factors into account it seems odd that our politicians persist in sending teenagers to war. Especially considering that the war they are fighting is not the remote target missile warfare we see on the TV, but on-the-ground warfare, with their mates getting blown to pieces right next to them.

'I am fortunate. I have not been in a position where my life has knowingly been in danger. I have never had to face the fear of walking or driving over a landmine. The closest I have been to harm is from a distressed patient trying to strangle me or patients spitting at me, unpleasant and distressing, but not life threatening. All my training in medicine and my experiences have given me mechanisms to cope with this level of threat. I still find it difficult. I cannot imagine, how, as a teenager I could cope with hours of boredom and waiting, followed by the gut wrenching terror of combat.

'When I do see ex-soldiers as patients I am impotent to help them cope with their PTSD, the level of emotional trauma is so far from normal experience that the usual NHS therapies are of little benefit. It is a tragedy that ex-service personnel end up on the streets or addicted to alcohol and drugs simply because the system has used them up and spat them out. Surely it is time to rethink how we wage our wars.'

The above is only an extract of Dr Cowley's letter, but I am sure that you will agree that there are some questions raised that need answering. On the TV programme *Return to the Falkland Islands* featuring former Welsh Guardsman Simon Weston, the subject of treating wounds, both physical and mental, was raised. Simon Weston said that he had received marvellous treatment as far as his physical wounds were concerned, but on the mental health side he was critical. Senior personnel replied, 'No, no, no, that's not right.' But Simon replied emphatically – 'We were ignored.'

DALEY, Cardinal Cahal Brendan

Archbishop of Armagh, Northern Ireland
Roman Catholic Primate of All Ireland 1990–1996

Cardinal Daley was considered 'the hierarchy's foremost theologian'. He strongly criticised the Irish Republican Army (IRA) throughout his long period of office as archbishop. He attracted global acclaim for writing the speech that Pope John Paul II gave on his 1979 visit to Drogheda in the Republic of Ireland to ask for an end to violence in Ireland. Cardinal Daley died in 2009.

'One of the great needs of our time is to deprive war of the "mythology" which has been cultivated concerning war – its glamour, its pageantry, its songs. We must "demythologise" war, we must tear off its attractive masks and reveal its evil, brutal, real face. War is a failure, however we glorify "victory". It is irrational, however sophisticated the technology – and however seductive the language of war.

'Let "never again to war" be our motto.'

DANNATT, Francis Richard GCB CBE MC DL

Chief of the General Staff 2006–2009
Constable of the Tower of London 2009

'General Sir Richard Dannatt is a soldier's soldier whose tenure as head of the Army has been marked by his willingness to embarrass the Government in defending his troops ... He recently called for more troops and helicopters in Afghanistan and influenced a reversal of the Government's decision to hold an Iraq war inquiry in private by telling ministers he saw "a lot of merit" in public hearings.' (*Daily Telegraph*, 17 July 2009.)

'For those who have never heard a shot fired in anger, war may seem a great adventure. After you have buried a few friends, you take a different view. How much better to spend time and effort in preventing conflict, than taking part in conflict.

The Wisdom of an Old Soldier'

DOBBS, Michael, Baron Dobbs of Wyle

Conservative MP 1986–1995
Chief of Staff of the Conservative Party 1986–1987

Michael Dobbs survived the Brighton Bombing in 1984. *The Guardian* dubbed him 'Westminster's baby-faced hit man' in the following year. He is the author of more than fifteen novels. In 2010 he was created a Life Peer, as Baron Dobbs of Wyle, in the County of Wiltshire. He sits on the Conservative benches in The House of Lords.

'Conflict The Fight for Freedom
Peace   Victory in the Fight for Freedom
Resolution Vigilance in the Fight for Freedom'

DODD, Kenneth 'Ken' Arthur

Stand- up comedian, TV star singer and actor

The legendary Ken Dodd has had nineteen Top 40 singles and sold over 1,000,000 copies of the single 'Tears'. In 1965, he was the UK's top-selling artist. He shared the stage with Kenneth Branagh in *Hamlet*.

'Congratulations on your current fundraising for Help for Heroes and Action Cancer.

'You asked for my thoughts on War, Peace, Conflict and Resolution. You have obviously received contributions from very eminent politicians and members of the public.

'I'm sure we all share a great sadness at the terrible loss of life as a result of the many conflicts that exist in the world today. Indeed the war on terrorism, of course, is world-wide. One would hope that the ease of communication between peoples of all countries via the internet and modern technology should improve the knowledge and understanding of different problems that exist between countries, and that many more situations should be resolved by peaceful means.

'Best wishes with the book and your fund raising efforts.'

DONALDSON, The Rt Hon Jeffrey

MP for Lagan Valley, Northern Ireland
Member of the Ulster Unionist Party until 2003
Member of the Democratic Unionist Party from 2003
Privy Councillor 2007

The Provisional IRA murdered two of Jeffrey Donaldson's cousins, both members of the RUC. Jeffrey joined the Ulster Defence Regiment at the age of 18.

'Conflict and Peace.

'For many years the people of Northern Ireland suffered dreadfully as a result of the divisions within our society and the actions of terrorists who were determined to pursue their evil agenda and to destroy the prospect of peace in our beloved province.

'However, the people of Northern Ireland never lost their will to achieve peace and it was their solid determination that brought about the triumph of hope over despair and the advent of The Peace Process. Reconciliation has been a key part of that process and this is a personal journey for each individual in coming to terms with the terrible things that may have happened in their lives and in their community. Healing can take many years and it is through the hope and prayers of our people that real peace will truly be realised in the fullness of time.'

ELLIOT, John

Former editor of Soldier *magazine*

Soldier magazine 'strives to offer an effective means of communication aimed primarily at junior ranks but also of interest to all ranks of the British Army, Cadets and the wider Military Community, including veterans and members of the public with an interest in militaria'.

> It is our privilege, not our duty, to remember the sacrifice of soldiers in war and peace.

ESSEX, David

Born David Albert Cook in 1947
Musician, singer, song-writer, actor

David Essex had nineteen Top 40 singles and sixteen Top 20 albums. He was voted No. 1 British Male Vocalist in 1974.

> My respect for those who fight and for those who fought, my sadness for those that have fallen, my wish is for Peace in the World.

FELLOWES, Julian Alexander, Baron Fellowes of West Stafford

Baron Kitchener-Fellowes of West Stafford is an actor, novelist, screenwriter, film director, producer and Conservative Peer. In 1999 he became Deputy Lord Mayor for Dorset. He is married to Emma Joy Kitchener LVO, Lady in Waiting to HRH Princess Michael of Kent, the great grandniece of Herbert Kitchener. Julian Fellowes is now of course best known as the creator of the TV drama series *Downton Abbey*.

> War is the curse of our existence. It also produces some of the greatest acts of courage and heroism that men and women are capable of. This is the paradox of war. The worst of times that brings out the best in us.

War is the curse of our existence. It also produces some of the greatest acts of courage and heroism that men and women are capable of. This is the paradox of war. The worst of times that brings out the best in us. *Julian Fellowes*

Sponsored by:
James Andrew Hall
Writer, TV Dramatist
01202 000000

FINNEGAN Colonel Terry

US Department of Defense
Central Command during Operation Desert Storm
Space Command and Defense Intelligence Agency
Author of Shooting the Front: Allied Aerial Reconnaissance in the First World War

> It is an indictment of civilization's progress when the surge of technological development comes when a nation is at war. If the energy that comes with conflict was applied to peaceful objectives serving mankind as a whole – a more meaningful experience could become a standard that embraces the purpose of existence.

CHRISTOPHER FINNEY: FRIENDLY FIRE

Christopher Finney, former Lance Corporal of Horse, Blues and Royals, was born in Brussels, Belgium, and was brought up in Stockport. He enlisted in the British Army in 2000. In 2003, he was serving with the Blues and Royals in Iraq when the Scimitar Armoured Vehicle he was driving came under attack from a pair of aircraft. Despite being wounded in the incident, he was able to rescue several of his comrades.

The attack was by ground Attack Aircraft of the United States Air Force. As this was an attack by a 'friendly force', under the rules of the award he was deemed not to qualify for a Victoria Cross because the attack had not been 'in the face of the enemy'.

He was awarded The George Cross and in doing so became the youngest serviceman in the British Armed Forces to receive it and the 154th recipient since its inception in 1940. His citation reads: 'During these attacks and their horrifying aftermath, Trooper Finney displayed clearheaded courage and devotion to his comrades which was out of all proportion to his age and experience.' The reward was made at Buckingham Palace by Her Majesty the Queen in 2004. He also received a special award at The Pride of Britain awards in 2004 in further recognition of his bravery. He was presented with an inscribed gold watch 'from the Citizens of Marple' to congratulate him on his 'deed of heroism'.

In 2009 he 'fell out of love' with the army and found work in a call centre in Poole. In an interview in a national newspaper he criticised the government and was offered a job as a 'Corporate Ambassador' by the Joe Calzaghe Enterprises Organisation. He now, along with his fiancée, Liz, and daughter, runs the Goonhaven Garden Centre in Cornwall.

FRANCIS GAUNT:
YOU HAVE TO LAUGH

If there is one thing more than anything else that links the services (and that includes the Fire Brigade, the Ambulance Service and the Police) it is humour. Humour amongst the Armed Services is special. It is 'sick', cruel, callous, black and very often controversial. It is that style of humour that enables soldiers on a daily basis to look at sometimes traumatic events and laugh at them, helping them to relax and cope.

Francis Gaunt was born in 1892 and joined the army at the age of 16 in 1908. In the First World War he was in the 16th Lancers and fought at Ypres, where he was bombed and gassed. He became a a prisoner of war for four years. At the end of hostilities he remained in the army and completed his service as a sergeant in the Irish Guards. He died whilst in the services and was buried with full military honours in 1929. This story about Sergeant Francis George Gaunt is told by his granddaughter.

'On being promoted, Francis was given the job of not only looking after, but also of training, the Regimental Mascot – a small puppy. They became great pals in everything except house training. This is where their friendship came into conflict with discipline. The problem was that the other soldiers spoilt the puppy and kept giving him scraps and tit-bits. The result was that "what went in one end had to come out of the other" and consequently grandfather was forever cleaning up. The problem had reached the ears of the sergeant major, who had already given two warnings to both the dog and keeper that "if there was one more incident, the dog would have to go". There followed a period of relative calm but this was short-lived. The final "accident" occurred in front of the regiment. The sergeant major went on the warpath and declared loudly, "Once more and out it will go via the vets to the great kennel in the sky."

'The morning of the ever-fraught barrack inspection came and everything was ship-shape. The RSM was about to leave the final bed space when he saw the mess on the floor and became apoplectic with rage, getting redder and redder, ranting and raving at my grandfather. He announced what was going to happen to the dog. My grandfather, rather insolently and forgetting his place, said, "But, please sir, we love this dog so much" and before anything else could be said, picked up the mess and ate it. There was silence and a look of sheer horror passed over the face of the RSM. For a while, to the men it seemed like an eternity, he was speechless. Eventually, in a calmer frame of mind but still stunned, he said, "If you love the bloody thing that much, you can bloody well keep it." With that he rushed out of the door before he was sick.

'There was a long pause, in case he was listening outside the door, and then the barrack room resounded with laughter. They knew if the RSM found out the puppy was still untrained all hell would break loose and life would be intolerable for everyone for an indefinite period. Fearing for the dog's future, a cunning plan had been hatched. Grandfather had fashioned a damp old piece of ginger cake into a suitable shape, laid it on the floor where it wasn't immediately visible and added a touch of water.

'It is unknown if the RSM was ever any the wiser, but the story spread and kept the morale of the troops high.'

TRAGEDY AT THE BARRACKS

'A Scottish soldier who accidentally shot dead a colleague in Northern Ireland has today [9 January 2003] been imprisoned for two years for manslaughter.'

The services are a dangerous place to work, even when not faced by the enemy. As an example, in the 1991 Gulf War, Iraqis killed 112 US troops and 180 Americans died from other causes, 35 by friendly fire and 145 in accidents. The loss is felt no less of course.

Shackleton Barracks, Ballykelly, Co Londonderry, 24 January 2001. Corporal Tony Green, Army Catering Corps, 25, died after being shot in the head when Private Graham's rifle discharged from the back of an army vehicle. The soldiers had been preparing to go on an operation in Co Fermanagh and Graham had placed his gun in the back of the vehicle. The operation was delayed and Cpl Green was returning to the cookhouse, and despite being 130 yards away when the gun went off, he was critically injured and died in Altnagelvin Hospital a day later.

Private Graham insisted he had put the safety catch on the weapon before putting it in the back of the vehicle and did not remember placing his finger on the trigger. Cpl Green was a married man and his wife was expecting a baby. Cpl Green's mother, Liz, said: 'Going to the barracks the next day my gut reaction was there was something very, very wrong.'

The following are words and thoughts of Cpl Green's aunt, Mrs Valerie Clark.

'My 25-year-old nephew Tony Green was killed in barracks in Northern Ireland in 2001. It was described as an "incident" by the MOD.

'To this day I watch my sister torture herself with unanswered questions. You brace yourself against hearing bad news when your loved ones are in the forces but do not expect safety in the barracks to be anything but 100%. Private Graham was a highly trained soldier and part of an elite group. We know the gun was not faulty. So, how could this happen? It did not happen on a shooting range; they were going out on a mission!'

The distraught mother, Mrs Liz Green:

'On 24 January 2001 at Shackleton Barracks, Northern Ireland, my 25-year-old son Corporal Tony Green was shot through the head, the bullet came from the rifle of Private Graham's rifle, who, we were told, was sitting in the back of a vehicle. Graham was later described in court as a highly trained soldier, the elite of the elite, a "marksman". Tony was taken to Altnagelvin Hospital; the life support machine was switched off the following day. How could anyone survive a bullet that had passed through the head from an SA80? How I felt at that time I cannot describe. I just remember feeling that something was wrong, gut reaction, mother's intuition, I do not know. My heart felt like it had been ripped out, but my lungs kept on taking in air and they were screaming why, why, why?

'In the early days I asked questions that were left either unanswered or the often given reply was "during the confusion". I remember thinking, what confusion? Tony's dead and nothing was making sense. I have sat through a five-day court case, read witness statements, asked questions of the powers-that-be and still feel that my questions have been left unanswered. There is one thing that is for certain, I miss Tony dearly; my other children have suffered terribly and miss their brother so much. I now have a 10-year-old grandson that never met his daddy. As a toddler, Dylan would point to Tony's photograph and say "that's my daddy". To the army, Tony was just a number that could be erased.

'I find it hard to go back to that time, it does not get easier, you just learn to live with the pain and the total isolation of losing a child in such tragic circumstances. Once I start thinking about it and put pen to paper I could write a book.

'So much happened in the four days I spent in Northern Ireland following Tony's death, and in the following years. I have asked so many questions, but still do not feel that I have had all the answers. I also feel that I have not heard the truth about what actually happened either on that day or the ones that followed. As the army would say, "They were confusing". Confusing to whom?'

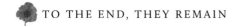

GUTHRIE, Charles Ronald Llewelyn GCB, LVO, OBE, DBL, DL,
Baron Guthrie of Craigiebank

Commands held: *1st Btn Welsh Guards*
                    4th Armoured Brigade
                    2nd Infantry Divison
                    1st British Corps
                    British Army of the Rhine
                    Chief of the General Staff
                    Chief of the Defence Staff

Baron Guthrie was appointed colonel commandant of the Intelligence Corps in 1986, colonel of the Life Guards and Gold Stick-in-Waiting to the Queen in 1999 and colonel commandant of the SAS Regiment in in 2000. He was promoted to the honorary rank of field marshal in June 2012.

The Armed Forces are the most loyal and respected part of
the fabric of state. We, and our government, forget this at
our peril. We should never forget what we owe them.

HAIN, Peter

Former Leader of the House of Commons and Secretary of State for Northern Ireland
Former Secretary of State for Wales

Peter Hain came to the UK from South Africa as a teenager and was a noted anti-apartheid campaigner in the 1970s. He retired from front-line politics in 2012.

Community, Care for others,
Compassion – the face of humanity.

HALL, James Andrew

Author, TV and film dramatist
Dramatisations: Prisoner of Zenda, Dombey and Son, Mill on the Floss, The Franchise Affair, Brat Farrar
Children's TV: Brendon Chase, Coral Island, Village By the Sea, The Bagthorpe Saga
Books (for children): The Curse of Brian's Brick, Fowl Pest
Books (for adults): Frost, Man in Aspic, Enemy at the Door
National Service Officer

‘ In a world that seldom seems to be without a war somewhere, let's be wise enough never to be on the side of the villains. ’

HILLS, William 'Billy'

Corporal, Section Commander, 1st Bn the Royal Regiment of Fusiliers
Awarded the Military Cross for action in Iraq in 2003

> It is an honour to know that a man has lain down his life for the sacred things in life and in the world, like his family, his friends, his country and for Peace. It is the work of a true man.

HEAD, Christopher

Captain, 1st Bn the Royal Regiment of Fusiliers
Awarded the Military Cross for Gallantry in Iraq in 2003 when a Lieutenant

> Peace, however uncertain, is always worth fighting for.

Lower Ballinderry Moravian Church
Card No. 3

"Peace, however uncertain, is always worth fighting for."

Captain C A Head MC

'Renewal Through Remembrance'
Sponsored by: Clarke Cunningham, (Tree Surgeon) 10 Ballytrim Rd., Killyleagh.
01396 828210 or 0860 787760.
Photograph by Roy Brown

HUGHES, Kim

Warrant Officer II, Royal Logistics Corps
Awarded the George Cross

'Raymond, what an outstanding gesture. Supporting these charities goes a long way. Often in my line of work I see the difference it makes to those in need. Your selfless act of giving is rarely seen these days. I'm sure your wife would be very proud.'
Kind regards, Kim Hughes GC

This was a card sent to me praising *my* selfless acts, but what have I done compared to his achievements? His actions were both selfless and brave. He saved the lives of others on military service. His actions are the backbone of our society. His actions earned him recognition from his fellow countrymen and women. (Kim is pictured on page 128.)

Extracts from the official citation:

'On 16 Aug 09, S/Sgt Hughes, along with a Royal Engineers Search Team were asked to provide close support to 2 Rifles Battlegroup during an operation to clear a route south-west of Sangin. Whilst conducting preliminary moves the point section initiated an IED resulting in a very serious casualty.

'During the casualty recovery the stretcher bearers initiated a second IED which resulted in two personnel being killed outright and four other very serious casualties, one of whom later died from his wounds.

'The area was effectively an IED minefield over-watched by the enemy and the section were stranded. Hughes and his team were called into this harrowing and chaotic scene to extract casualties and recover bodies. On reaching the first injured soldier, Hughes discovered a further IED, which constituted a further threat to the lives of the casualties. Hughes carried out a manual neutralisation of the IED. This was a Category A situation which is only carried out if it is suspected an IED may be attached to an individual and where a mass casualty event may occur if not carried out. Hughes went on to neutralise two further IEDs. His utterly selfless action allowed the casualties to be extracted and the bodies recovered. The team discovered a further four IEDs and disposed of them also.'

To dispose of seven IEDS using manual neutralisation is the most outstanding act of explosive ordnance disposal ever recorded in Afghanistan.

HAYMAN, The Right Honourable Baroness Hélène Valerie GBE PC

Privy Council member 2001
Speaker of the House of Lords 2006–2011
Member of the House of Lords 1996
Created Baroness Hayman of Dartmouth Park in the London Borough of
*   Camden in 1996*
Member of Parliament 1974–1979
In 2006 she won the inaugural election for the newly created position of
*   Lord Speaker*

> Conflict is a means to the end, it is not a justification. We must continue to try and find a dialogue that will bring about a peaceful solution. There is no 'victor' in conflict, we all lose.

HISTORY STUDENT

Mature history student, Northern Ireland
Anonymous

The point made here is his and his alone, and he wishes to remain anonymous. This individual was born, raised and educated in Northern Ireland and does a tremendous amount of work for both his immediate community and the wider international community. He has been awarded an MBE.

'Whilst I joined in the euphoria of the Peace Agreement being signed and agreed by the political leaders of the USA, the UK and The Republic of Ireland, I believe that they, the people, are still in a state of doomed compromise. As the wheels of history continuously show, there will always be a minority who will never accept either defeat or compromise. Until the objectives of the minority are met then conflict will return and this will, inevitably, lead to even more conflict.

'Looking at my family through the generations I recall that my parents and grandparents lived and worked through times of conflict in their own neighbourhoods. I myself have lived and worked through the "Troubles". My children have also lived through them and now accept it as a basic fact of life. I now believe my grandchildren will also grow up with that same acceptance and consider it normal.

'An "arranged marriage" is how I see the current situation, and, although the pot may be off the boil, it is still simmering away.'

OTTO HORNUNG: REFUGEE, COLONEL

'The Nazis took my youth.
The Russians took my freedom.
The British saved me.'

Otto's Jewish family living in Czechoslovakia when the Germans annexed the country knew that restrictions would soon be applied. His father, Ernst, devised a plan where Otto, dressed as a postman, would escape across the border into Poland to a relative. Poland at that time had not been occupied. When war broke, out Otto went to the British Embassy in Krakow and volunteered to join the British Army. As there was no foreign fighting force at that time, he was refused. At age 18, he and a group of expatriate Czechs

had been captured on the way to Romania by the Russians and interned in Russia for 18 months. He finally made his way to Romania, where he joined with a band of expatriate Czechs as a resistance fighter and eventually linked up with the Russian forces.

Meanwhile his father, Ernst, who had also escaped to Poland, was to meet the same fate as many thousands of other Jews. Deported to Nisko he escaped, was recaptured and shot.

His mother and sister were determined to join a family relative in Hungary but needed a permit from the Gestapo commandant to leave Czechoslovakia. His mother dressed herself in her very best finery and presented herself to the commandant. He replied that he would give them a permit simply because he admired her courage. They made their way to Hungary, where she acquired a Swedish passport from the celebrated diplomat Raoul Wallenberg, who, it was recognised after the war, had saved something approaching 100,000 Jews from certain death in Hungary.

Otto eventually joined the British Army and saw service in Tobruk, Dunkirk and Normandy, reaching the rank of colonel. At the end of the war he was repatriated to Czechoslovakia, where he lived under communist rule for twenty-two years. He escaped and headed for the country he loved, but had never seen and arrived in London in 1967.

He weeps as he describes the feeling of finally landing on British soil. He said, 'Finally, I had come home.'

Otto became president of the International Association of Philatelic Journalists and travelled all over the world talking and judging philatelic competitions and exhibitions. At one exhibition in Stockholm he was sitting next to another judge, Mr Emil Mewes, a German, and the subject of the war arose. Otto mentioned that he had been fighting in Tobruk, and Mr Mewes jumped with shock and replied, 'Oh, were you? Me too.' Otto replied, 'Yes, but I was on the other side!' They went on to become great friends and continued judging exhibits around the world. Otto is pictured, centre, at an international philatelic exhibition in Stockhom in 1974; Emil Mewes is on the right, ex US serviceman Charles Peterson on the right.

HART DYKE, Captain David, CBE LVO RN

In 1982 Captain Hart Dyke was commanding HMS *Coventry* during the Falklands conflict. A helicopter from the ship attacked and sank an Argentine naval vessel, and soon after the ship had destroyed several enemy helicopters and aircraft. On 25 May she was attacked by four Argentine aircraft and was hit by three bombs and sank the following day. Nineteen of her crew were lost and thirty injured. One of the wounded, Paul Mills, suffered from complications from a skull fracture sustained in the sinking of the ship and died on 29 March 1983.

> My life and commitment to the Royal Navy has been rewarded by its major role in peace-keeping and representing Britain's interest overseas. The RN aims to prevent war through diplomacy. Only in the last resort should arms be used. But, when we have to, the RN is very good at fighting if the cause is just.

HOLDEN, Amanda Louise

Actress, singer and presenter

'I never see the point of war, lives are lost and it brings nothing but horrendous pain and worry to the families of the men that serve.
However, my involvement with 'The Millie Awards' [*The Sun*'s annual military awards] every year has forced me to see the courage, bravery and heroics in all who serve our country.
They all make me proud to be British.'

JAMES, Margot

Vice Chairman of the Conservative Party 2000–2010

'I think that it is important that remembrance and reflection on those that have given their lives in the service of our country is facilitated in schools.
I went to a boarding school and we had to watch The Remembrance Day Service. A good thing too. My father volunteered for active service in the Second World War.
He didn't have to as he was in a protected industry.
The coal trade. He served in India for three and a half years. I am very proud of both my parents and of the sacrifices they made for our freedom.'

JACKSON, General Sir Michael ('Mike') David
GCB CBE DSO ADC DL

Commissioned into the Intelligence Corps
1984: Commanding Officer, Parachute Regiment
Commander British Forces NI
1994:Commander multinational Division, Balkans
Commander NATO Quick Reaction Forces

General Mike Jackson was chief of the General Staff from 2003 to 2006. The press nicknamed him 'Macho Jacko'. From the Intelligence Corps via the Parachute Regiment and the events of 'Bloody Sunday' in 1972 to head of the British Army at the outbreak of the Iraq War, he served for forty-five years.

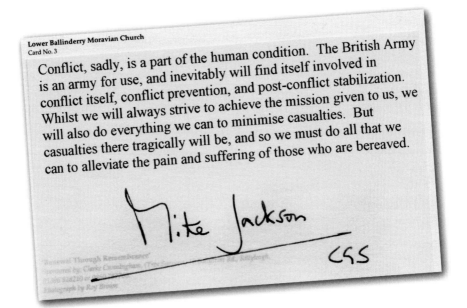

Lower Ballinderry Moravian Church
Card No. 3

Conflict, sadly, is a part of the human condition. The British Army is an army for use, and inevitably will find itself involved in conflict itself, conflict prevention, and post-conflict stabilization. Whilst we will always strive to achieve the mission given to us, we will also do everything we can to minimise casualties. But casualties there tragically will be, and so we must do all that we can to alleviate the pain and suffering of those who are bereaved.

Mike Jackson

CGS

KELLY, Matthew

Actor, presenter

'Many thanks for your letter, and it was fascinating to read about "War, Peace and Reconciliation".

'I was incredibly moved during a short film I made for the television programme *My Family at War*, when I traced what had happened to my Great Uncle Albert during the First World War and finally was able to put flowers on his grave which we found in Germany. It made me understand and appreciate much more the strength and bravery shown by my Dad Ron, who was a very young man during the Second World War and went to Normandy in his landing craft. I asked him some years ago which of the beaches he went to and he replied "All of them." He and his landing craft and crew landed 26 times during the D-Day landings. I cannot begin to imagine the terror he felt, and courage he, and all the other participants, showed, that day. Ordinary people doing extra-ordinary things.

'Good luck with the book, and with raising money for Help for Heroes, and for Action Cancer.'

LYNN, Dame Vera, DBE

Singer, actress
'The Forces Sweetheart'

Vera Lynn travelled to many battle-fronts to entertain the troops and boost the morale of our service personnel during the Second World War. She became known as 'The Forces Sweetheart', and brought tears to many eyes with her songs of home and family, such as 'We'll Meet Again' and 'The White Cliffs of Dover'. A little-known fact is that she was the first British female artist to top the American charts. In 2010, she released an album of her wartime hits, and this sold over 1,000,000 copies in the United Kingdom alone, thus making her the oldest artist to have a No. 1 hit in the album charts.

> It is good that we have Remembrance Day, as it is good we never forget those who gave their lives for us and continue to do so.

Lower Ballinderry Moravian Church
Card No. 3

It is good we still have remembrance day, as it is good we never forget those who gave their lives for us. and continue to do so.

Vera Lynn

'Renewal Through Remembrance'
Sponsored by: Clarke Cunningham, (Tree Surgeon) 10 Ballytrim Rd., Killyleagh.
01396 828210 or 0860 787760.
Photograph by Roy Brown

LUMLEY, Joanna, OBE FRGS

Actress, model, activist

Joanna Lumley is an actress, comedienne, model, campaigner and author. Born in Srinagar in the state of Kashmir, her father was Major James Rutherford Lumley, who served in the 6th Ghurkha Rifles. She works for the Ghurkha Justice Campaign and Survival International and is a patron of Tree Aid and PENHA (Pastoral and Environmental Network in the Horn of Africa).

Give Peace a Chance

As the daughter of a professional soldier I know sometimes peace can only be won by conflict – peace is the most precious flower, growing on the same tree as freedom, compassion and loving kindness. If you ever have to choose between war and peace, give peace a chance first. Try in every way to find a peaceful solution. Keep trying: and when all seems lost, try again, and fight for it if you have to.

"Give Peace a Chance".

MURIEL MAGEE, A MOTHER'S VOICE

Muriel Magee lives in Northern Ireland and has written several poems that have been published in various anthologies, one of which is published here. Muriel considers the experiences of her family as 'normal' and no different from anyone else's.

She recalls that she had two cousins serving with the Police in Northern Ireland; both were living within their local communities. One was living in the village of Coalisland in County Tyrone when an attempt was made on his life. Gunmen opened fire on his house one evening. It was fortunate that at the time the family were not at home, but permanent changes had to be made to their whole lifestyle. Another cousin was living in the Republican town of Crossmaglen when he was 'warned off' that he was to be 'targeted'. He now

lives in England, but to this day he hates seeing the sign saying 'Crossmaglen'
when he visits. Maureen's brother was commissioned into the army and rose
to the rank of lieutenant colonel but was forced to leave Northern Ireland
because of his 'high risk value'.

Muriel and her family consider themselves quite ordinary, like so many
others; they have given so much for freedom, for the people and the country.

The Conflict

The war broke out in '69
On the street civil rights
Were found
Our excuse to the world
As Church and State,
If we had only known
What was our fate?

Far too many years
We have struggled with war
Everyone living in dread and fear
The pain, the grief
That we have suffered from loss
Headstones already gathering moss.

As we lay our dead side by side
We keep asking the same question
'In God's name why have they died?'
If only the key to the conflict be found
Perhaps our leaders will all sit round
And bring this land, so torn apart
Back to the peace we knew at the start.

MARR, Colonel Simon, MBE

Commanding Officer
1st Battalion the Royal Regiment of Fusiliers
Awarded the MBE for service in Iraq

One of the duties of a CO is of course to communicate messages such as this one, about Sergeant John Jones, who was killed by a roadside bomb in Iraq on 20 November 2005. Lt Col Simon Marr:

'Sergeant John Jones' tragic and untimely death has come as an immense blow and shock to his immediate family, his friends and all members of the Royal Regiment of Fusiliers. "Jonah" Jones was a much loved and highly popular member of our Battalion, the First Fusiliers. Brimming with energy, a love of soldiering and an endearing sense of humour and compassion for his men, he will be sorely missed. Whether it was on operations or during training with the soldiers he led so ably, or on the sports field or in the boxing ring, he showed remarkable qualities of professionalism, grit and absolute determination. Having already completed a tour of Iraq in March 2003, he looked forward with optimism and determination to playing his part in

Lower Ballinderry Moravian Church
Card No. 3

I feel honoured and privileged to command men and women whose role is to bring peace and stability to those in need.

We must never forget the ultimate sacrifice that our soldiers may be called upon to make in order to achieve peace in times of conflict.

Lt Col SIMON MARR MBE KXF
Commanding First Fusiliers

'Renewal Through Remembrance'
Sponsored by: Clarke Cunningham, (Tree Surgeon) 10 Ballytrim Rd., Killyleagh.
01396 828210 or 0860 787760.
Photograph by Roy Brown

bringing a semblance of stability and normality to Iraq. In the short period of this tour, he and his patrol had already established an excellent rapport with the local population and he was enjoying the challenges of his role.

'Sergeant Jones was an outstanding soldier, a wonderful husband and a loving father, who always found time to speak to and encourage those around him. He had a smile for everyone. We are left remembering his drive, his courage, his humour and his typically understated contribution to the Battalion. We will never forget him.'

'I was honoured and privileged to command men and women whose role it is to bring peace and stability to those in need.
We must never forget the ultimate sacrifice that our soldiers are called upon to make in order to achieve peace in times of conflict.'

McCONNELL, Jack,
Baron McConnell of Glenscorrodale

Privy Councillor, MSP
First Minister of Scotland 2001–2007

'My generation owe those who fought in the Second
World War a debt for the peace we have enjoyed.
Those that have never been placed at the heart
of conflict should never forget those who made a
sacrifice then and in other wars since.'

McKENNA, Virginia, OBE

Stage and screen actress

Virginia McKenna won a BAFTA Award for Best Actress in 1956 for *A Town Like Alice* and was Oscar-nominated for her role as Violette Szabo in the film *Carve Her Name with Pride*. She is best known for her 1966 role as Joy Adamson in the true-life film *Born Free*, for which she won a Golden Globe.

She and her late husband, Bill Travers, who also starred with her in *Born Free*, became wild animal rights campaigners and fought for the protection of their natural habitat. They set up a conservation area in Kenya, which also became their home. In 2004, she was awarded the Order of the British Empire in recognition of her services to wildlife and the arts.

'When I think about wars and all that they mean, various thoughts and emotions arise. Perhaps one of the strongest is a source of overwhelming gratitude to the many extraordinary men and women prepared to risk their lives. I do not always feel these sacrifices are justified, as we sometimes seem to be involved in wars in remote places for remote reasons. So I feel deeply sad about those, as many families lose treasured sons and daughter, husbands and brothers in conflicts they do not fully understand or believe are warranted. I am against violence of all kinds, and therefore I never lose hope that one day guns will be silenced, hatred and distrust will end and kindness, respect and love will triumph.'

MORGAN, Hywel Rhodri

Retired as First Minister for Wales December 2009
Chancellor of Swansea University 2011
Rhodri Morgan is a committed supporter of Welsh devolution.

> I was a Blitzkrieg baby. I was born in September
> 1939 just as Germany was smashing its way across
> Poland. My mother said to the owner of the nursing
> home, "I've read about the Blitzkrieg, shouldn't we
> be in the basement and not the attic?"
> The landlady replied, "Don't you worry now my
> dear, these old Cardiff houses are built very solidly!"
> How can anyone know what war is like,
> unless you've been there?

MORRIS, Raymond,
Laird of Balgorrie and Eddergoll

'War, when required to defend our country is justified, but certainly not when politically motivated as at present. Some politicians should be charged with crimes against their country. Once upon a time, terrorism was a national problem, but now, interfering politicians have caused it to become a horror of global proportions.

'My father fought through WWI with the Royal Naval Division and was mustard-gassed in the trenches, though not fatally. I served with the Gordon Highlanders for my National Service in 1948 and was involved with the Berlin Airlift.

'May God help us all in the future.'

MOUNTBATTEN, Patricia,
2nd Countess Mountbatten of Burma CBE MSC CD JP DL

Lord Mountbatten KG, GCB, OM, GCSI, GCIE, GCVO, PC, FRS was murdered at age 79 by the IRA in August 1979, when they blew up *Shadow V*, an old fishing boat, in the Republic of Ireland. His grandson, the Hon Nicholas Knatchbull (14) and local Irish boy Paul Maxwell (15) also died. Lord Mountbatten's 83-year-old mother, the Dowager Lady Braeburn, died twenty-four hours later. Lord Mountbatten's daughter, Patricia, her husband, Lord Braeburn and their other son, the Hon Timothy Knatchbull, were all hospitalised with various injuries.

Patricia Mountbatten succeeded to her father's title when he was assassinated. The inheritance accorded her the title of countess and a seat in the House of Lords, where she remained until 1999, when the House of Lords Act 1999 removed most hereditary peers from the House. The Countess was colonel in chief of Princess Patricia's Canadian Light Infantry until 2007. That year, the governor general of Canada presented her with a Canadian Meritorious Service Medal.

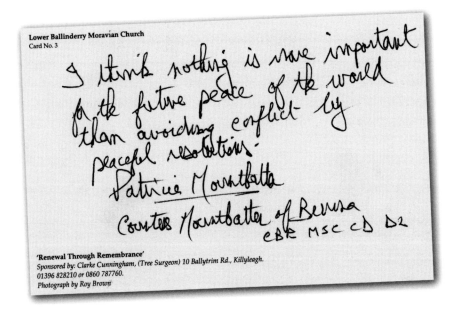

Lower Ballinderry Moravian Church
Card No. 3

I think nothing is more important for the future peace of the world than avoiding conflict by peaceful resolution.
Patricia Mountbatten
Countess Mountbatten of Burma CBE MSC CD DL

'Renewal Through Remembrance'
Sponsored by: Clarke Cunningham, (Tree Surgeon) 10 Ballytrim Rd., Killyleagh.
01396 828210 or 0860 787760.
Photograph by Roy Brown

MULHERN Regimental Sergeant Major,
1st Btn the Royal Regiment of Fusiliers

RSM Mulhern was awarded the MBE (Mil) for service in Iraq.

> One can only really appreciate the stability of peace after having experienced the turmoil of conflict.

NORTHUMBERLAND, His Grace The Duke of

Alnwick Castle in Northumberland is the home of the Percy family and is also the home of the Royal Northumberland Fusiliers Regimental Museum. The Duke is an honorary Colonel of the Royal Regiment of Fusiliers, and one of the Regimental Battalions has its own Northumbrian piper, who is normally a member of the band.

The Percy family's burial place is Westminster Abbey; they are the last family to maintain this tradition.

> Away from the action, it is easy to shut our eyes and minds to the bravery and sacrifice made by our armed forces to protect us and our way of life. Those who die in battle are remembered forever on memorial stones. For those whose lives are changed forever, physically or mentally wounded, we must ensure that they too are remembered so that they can live their lives without suffering.

CAPTAIN PETER NORTON GC: IN COMMAND, IN CONTROL

The George Cross Citation as it appeared in the *London Gazette*:

'Captain Norton was the second-in-command of the US Combined Explosive Exploration Cell based on the outskirts of Baghdad. The unit has been in the forefront of counter Improvised Explosive Device Operations and it plays a vital role in the collection and analysis of weapons intelligence.

'At 1917hrs on 24 July 2005, a three-vehicle patrol from B Coy, 2nd Btn 121st Regiment of the Georgia National Guard was attacked by a massive command-initiated IED in the Al Bayaa district of Baghdad. The explosion resulted in the deaths of 4 US Servicemen. Due to the significance of the explosion Captain Norton lead a team immediately to the scene. On arrival he faced a scene of carnage and the inevitable confusion that it causes. He quickly took charge and was informed that a possible command wire had been spotted in the area of the explosion. Captain Norton instructed the team and US service personnel to remain with their vehicle while he alone went forward to confirm if the command wire was present.

'A short while later, an explosion occurred and Captain Norton sustained a traumatic amputation of his left leg and suffered serious blast and fragmentation to his right leg, arms and lower abdomen. When his team came forward to render first aid he was lucid, conscious and concerned about their safety. He initially refused first aid until he was sure the team were safe. Despite having sustained grievous injuries he remained in command and directed follow up actions. Captain Norton told them the areas where it was safe to move to and a further device was found ten metres away. His presence and clear orders in the most difficult circumstances prevented further serious injury or loss of life.'

THE NUN WHO RISKED HER LIFE

The following contributor is in a religious order and wishes to remain anonymous.

'I was in a convent in Belgium as the Germans were marching through Europe and they had promised the people of the country a Christmas present that they would not forget. They carried out that threat and the present came in the form of bombing raids between the hours of 8pm and 9am. There were a lot of dead on the streets. Bodies were everywhere and loved ones could be seen wandering round trying to identify them. It was a dreadful and pitiable sight. We had heard stories and seen for ourselves what was happening to the Jews of the city. We took several Jewish girls and hid them from the Nazis and prayed that we would never be found out.

'The German soldiers used to ring the convent bell at 3am and we had to get up and make a hot meal for them. We could not say no, because of the girls in hiding and because of what we knew had happened to villagers and farmers who refused. One day German soldiers were marching past the convent and one very young soldier asked for a drink of water, he was also in pain because his feet were covered in blisters and were raw from ill-fitting boots. As a nurse I offered to bandage them but he told me that if he was to stop he would be beaten until he either got up or dropped.'

In recent years the sister has been acknowledged for her bravery and compassion by the Vatican, and all she could say in a very modest way was: 'It was a very frightening time for all of us. All we could do was to pray to the Lord they did not catch us. We took risks but God was with us. I drew on my faith because if we do not have faith, then we have nothing.'

OSGOOD, Alan

Retired Ship's Officer, P & O

'At the outbreak of the Second World War I was nine years old and lived near the RAF station at Hornchurch in Essex. I remember playing in the "zig-zag" trenches dug in nearby fields, so that they could practise trench warfare. With a friend I used to go out looking for pieces of German aircraft that had been shot down, and when we found something that was not being guarded, we would fight over whatever it was. On one occasion I won, but in doing so my friend dropped whatever it was and I fell on it. To this day I still have a scar on my left hand.

'School was disrupted and lessons were carried out in the teacher's house. Either that or we collected work to do at home or in the shelter at the bottom of the garden. Sitting in the shelter, using a torch or an oil lantern, we could hear the loud crack of an ack-ack gun, which we called "Whalebone Annie" because it was sited on Whalebone Road.

'A land mine fell across the road about 100 yards from our house on some allotments but failed to go off. The story went that the parachute had been seen but everyone thought that it was "Old Joe" liming his patch. At daylight it was realised it was a mine that had been dropped by parachute and was very dangerous. We were rushed off and evacuated while it was defused to a local school, great excitement.

'I was good at aircraft recognition and often saw American aircraft flying over returning from daylight raids, some with stopped engines, some with gently trailing smoke. Most were Flying Fortresses, Liberators or Marauders. One cloudy day there was a loud explosion in the sky and the combustion chamber/jet pipe of a V2 rocket fell from the sky. It demolished the garage of a nearby house and my brother and I cycled round to see the damage.

'I remember my father being away from home a lot. He was Marine Superintendent for the Blue Star Line and was responsible for their ships around the South Coast of the UK, which stretched from Bristol to Middlesborough. My uncle went into the 16/5th Lancers and eventually saw action in Africa and Italy. I remember feeling sad when he came to our home to say that he was off to war.

'Even going to the local shop for a newspaper was exciting, especially when I thought that an enemy Me109 was shooting at me. In reality the enemy plane had been attacking nearby Romford Gas Works and was being chased by a Spitfire who was firing at him. The shell cases were dropping to the ground around me so I thought it was me being attacked.

'Later I went with my father to the dockyards in London and somehow I was left on the dockside with some dockworkers when the docks were attacked. We ran and hid under a lift bridge until the all clear was sounded.

'I do recall that as a young boy, life was exciting. After all, I was only nine when it started and fourteen when it finished. But at the same time it could be, and was, very frightening. You created your own adventure.'

OSGOOD, Judith (Hall)

Retired Senior Radiographer
Hospital volunteer

'I was nearly seven years old when the Second World War broke out. We were on holiday near Cromer in Norfolk with another family. It was thought that the East coast might be invaded, so two families, each with two children and both mothers pregnant, crammed into a small car (there was a mattress strapped to the roof so any bombs dropped would bounce off!) and we drove to Wales. As far away as we could go. We spent a few months in a rented house and then moved to Blackpool before settling in Troon, Scotland, for a couple of years.

'My father was a Medical Officer in the Royal Air Force at Prestwick. I remember having two teeth taken out by the Royal Air Force Dentist. At the age of eight I went to a boarding school in Malvern – I wore an identity disc with my name and identity number. The number later became my NHS number.

'At the age of eleven I went to another boarding school in Norfolk. The army had just returned the school after several years of occupation. It was in dire need of redecoration (there were several notices in our dormitories saying, "If in need, call a mistress" – I am not sure if that was for our benefit or for the army's!).

'When at home during the holidays we slept in a brick air raid shelter attached to the house. There were raids every night. Sometimes during the daytime we saw our fighters trying to shoot down V1 rockets (doodle bugs) over the sea, before they managed to hit land. We used to get food parcels from relatives in New Zealand with tins of butter – lard – honey and fruit-cake. This caused great excitement. Food rationing went on for some years after the war ended. As I was tall and had big feet I was entitled to extra clothing coupons.

'When my father was demobbed he came home with new underwear that looked like wartime bread: a flecked appearance of white and brown, also bleached towels that I am still using.

'Now many years later I feel very strongly that there would be no wars if women were in charge. Nurturing a child through pregnancy only to have it killed later in a religious or political conflict is both devastating and a terrible waste.'

PAISLEY, Dr Reverend Ian, MP MLA

1971 – 2008	*Democratic Unionist Party*
1970 – 2010	*Member of Parliament*
1977	*Opposed the Sunningdale Agreement*
1979 – 2004	*Member of the European Parliament*
1985	*'Ulster Says No' to Anglo-Irish Agreement*
1988	*Opposed the Belfast Agreement*
1998 – 2011	*MLA*
2010	*Created a Life Peer, Lord Bannside*

John Hume MP once said to Ian Paisley, 'If, the word "no" was removed from the English language, you'd be speechless wouldn't you?' Ian Paisley replied, 'No. I wouldn't.'

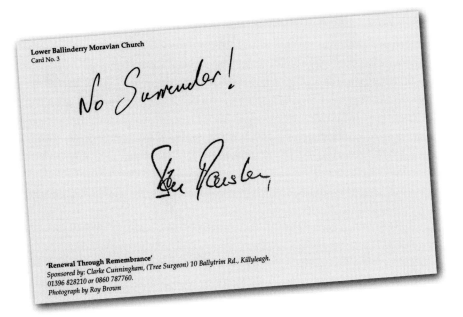

PARRY, Colin

Father of Tim Parry, killed by the IRA in Warrington

On 20 March 1993 police received a coded warning at 11.58hrs that a bomb had been planted outside Boots in Liverpool; but the bombs went off near Boots in Warrington, sixteen miles away. At 12.12 the first of the bombs went off. They had been planted in cast-iron litterbins, which had the effect of turning them into huge hand grenades There had been no time to evacuate the area after Merseyside police informed the Cheshire force of the warning.

Jonathan Ball, 3, died in the blasts when he was in town with his babysitter buying a Mother's Day Card. Tim Parry, 12, was caught by the full force of the blast and died five days later in hospital. The atrocity left fifty-six people injured.

Mr and Mrs Parry are victims of terrorism.

Mr and Mrs Ball are victims of terrorism.

Colin and Wendy Parry set up 'The Foundation for Peace', which is the only charitable organisation that supports victims and survivors of acts of terrorism through the provision of learning programmes that explore the causes and effects of conflict and its resolution through non-violent means. The Tim Parry–Jonathan Ball Young People's centre was opened seven years after the tragedy. It is run by the NSPCC and the Tim Parry–Jonathan Ball Trust and includes residential accommodation for visiting groups from Ireland and around the world.

> 'Conflict is overwhelmingly neutralised by frequent laughter which inspires compromise and togetherness.'

It is a card that should make each and everyone of us think: 'What would I say if I lost a child in such circumstances?'

In 2007 Sinn Féin president Gerry Adams made a keynote address at a special event in London organised in aid of the Foundation for Peace. 'Irish republicans – the IRA – were responsible for what happened that day. It brought huge grief to these two families, as well as to others hurt in that incident. The IRA expressed its regret at what had happened. In 2002 it apologised to all those non-combatants it had killed or injured and their families. I have also expressed my personal and sincere regret, and apologised for the hurt inflicted by Republicans. I do so again this evening.'

THE PRIESTS

The Priests are a classical musical group made up of three Catholic priests from Northern Ireland. They consist of brothers Fr Martin and Fr Eugene O'Hagan and Fr David Delargy.

In 2008 they won the award for the fastest-selling debut classical record. Their first LP sold over 1,000,000 copies and has earned them a Gold Disc. They have appeared in front of royalty, presidents and the pope.

Father Martin O'Hagan:

'Peace is the result of seeds sown in the past, may we have the courage to be sowers of seeds for the present and the future.'

Father Eugene O'Hagan:

'My soul is longing for your peace – near to you my God.'

Father David Delargy:

'Peace I leave you
My own peace I give you
A peace the world cannot give
That is my gift to you.'

PEACE PROTESTORS, LONDON

In 2010 I made a very rare visit to London, initially to see the sights. I went to the Houses of Parliament and was greeted with a sight that was beyond comprehension. Parliament Green appeared to have been taken over by hippies; anti this and anti that and banners and bunting proclaiming 'Human Rights for All'; 'Get Britain out of Iraq'; 'Get Britain out of Afghanistan'; 'Bring Our Troops Home'; 'No More Killing'. Watching all this were the photo-snapping tourists and the photo-snapping police.

I was fascinated and immediately thought that the opinions of some of those demonstrating may be of interest for this book, especially bearing in mind those Afghanistan and Iraq banners. Were the demonstrators anti-troops?

With apprehension I approached some of them, watched by 'Big Brother'. In fact, they were intelligent, polite and up-to-date with events. They had talked to servicemen who had also visited them when on leave, and there had only been one case of public disorder. I took some photographs, and two of the demonstrators agreed to complete cards with their thoughts.

'It is more important now in this time not to be afraid of any force we do not know. Know the force; do not make it your enemy. Identify the enemy within and make it your friend and give that friend love in more ways than you have ever done before.

Peace in the Heart is freedom

Freedom is life and Love.'

Dawn Evans

'If all the energy that is used for destruction was used for healing, and the only profit that we aimed to achieve was a better future for all, if our energies were used to help all around, then, through will, we will be able to realise Heaven on Earth.

The choice is there for all

The will is yours

To realise peace is to start to heal the world.'

Anon

'P' – Northern Ireland

'I am now 36 years old, and have my own house in Belfast, with a mortgage still being paid for. I have a happy life, I have an honest job and get a few holidays every year, but why am I here in Northern Ireland? Quite simple really, Belfast is my home, born and bred.

'From recent travels I realize how much there is to learn about other cultures and traditions in our world. A recent trip to China proved to me that different cultures and life can be led according to who runs the country. I have seen conflict in other countries and so much pain and hurt in the world and, sadly, it makes me realise that I can relate to it. My past is maybe unusual.

'Conflict in Belfast in the early 1970s was dangerous, and my grandparents made the decision to move away, to Dublin. My future mother had at the time a promising career as a nurse and decided to stay in Belfast on her own. A difficult decision. Her parents left, she stayed. She had a great career, she met a man, my Dad.

'Dublin became the framework for the family. An uncle in Dublin owned a factory and I had my first summer job as a teenager at this factory. Values were learnt and I was being taught about life and how to accept prejudice – all I did was to work in a great job for my uncle, I packed boxes, got orders out on time – I enjoyed it. It was a summer job. Abuse came from other workers because they felt I came from a different religion, they assumed wrongly that because I was from the North that I was not the same as them – (I was same family and same religion as my uncle, but from the North) so there was aggression from the staff. It was the first time I had really experienced this type of – what – bullying? Not sure what to call it, maybe it was just a misunderstanding of differences of religion, I accepted those differences but they did not. It was real, it was all around me. I was young and it could have influenced me for good or bad, I did not let it do the latter.

'I let myself find my own beliefs and I have found that I had a strong (sometimes strict) upbringing, but the result is me, and I am proud of being me. I know I can rise above any petty comments about religion or political types and have my own mind. I have tried to learn from every side before making my decisions. Everyone deserves an equal chance, so if we all learned before making our decisions I think it would make us all better people.

'The young lads that I worked with in Dublin in the factory thought that because I came from Belfast that I had been going to school dodging bullets every day, if I were to tell them today or if they read this, they might now believe me that I did not.

'10 April 1998. The signing of the Good Friday Agreement, otherwise known as the Belfast Agreement. This was a momentous day. This was an occasion for celebration, but ...

There are still guns on the streets.

Still men on release from prisons on licence who should not be.

'The City Mayor, a member of Sinn Féin, would allegedly stand down to avoid meeting the Queen on her Diamond Jubilee visit.

'A while later I was passing through Belfast City Centre and as big as the news was, I was not overly impressed or bothered either way. A lot of locals like myself just thought, "Oh, another decision made by people in power" – we have sadly got used to a system where so many people from different sides make decisions and then an "agreement" is struck. Decommissioning? A great idea, only if both sides are honest. And I think everyone in the whole country knows that if you want to win a war then you still need to have a back up! (I am not taking sides but just stating a fact.) This was a major news event, television crews from around the world, something to be remembered. We walked to the Waterfront Conference Centre where it was all happening and, to my horror, I was caught like a deer in headlights by a television camera. Who would see me? Where was it being shown? I answered the interviewer's first question, "Why was I there?" I replied that I lived there and wanted to know what was going on. With a camera in my face, she asked me, "How did I feel about the changes in my country?"

'Then I came alive, I let it all go, and I really surprised myself. (Yes, me, the quiet guy – the author will vouch for that.)

'I said, "I have lived my whole life knowing nothing but war and deaths caused by groups of people who cannot agree on insignificant differences. Give peace a chance and let everyone realize that no one is winning. No one wants any more killing, we have had enough."

'This was my way of life, and she was told that – a plain matter of fact. The TV camera guy got it all, then leaned to her and said, "That's it – perfect," not "cut" like in the films but she understood and turned to me with a tear in her eyes and said, "That was perfect."

'I often wondered where that footage was shown and would love to see it but I will always think that I (in a small way), have become part of our history and it is on camera and in storage somewhere for the future. That is my story, and my small part in the "Troubles".'

PUTTNAM, David,
Baron Puttnam of Queensgate

Film Director: The Mission, Killing Fields, Chariots of Fire, Local Hero

> If every child were taught to appreciate and respect all opinions, if every child were treated with kindness and consideration, we would gradually see the extinction of the bully in society and those who presume to force their beliefs on the world's people.

Sold in aid of:
Help 4 Heroes
Action Cancer

If every child were taught to appreciate and to respect all opinions. If every child were treated with kindness and Consideration; we would gradually see the extinction of the bully in Society and those who presume to force their beliefs on the world's people.

David Puttnam

Sponsored by:
John Turner (Bournemouth)
Ex 32 Heavy Regt. R.A.

REES, Tim, Welsh Guards

With the 1st Battalion Welsh Guards Tim saw active service in Northern Ireland and the Falklands war of 1982. During peacetime, his duties included battalion photographer, a job that included covering many historical and royal events. His regular 'bivouak' for the night when in London was Buckingham Palace! Upon leaving the army, he went to work for the BBC in Cardiff. He was asked to tell his story of the war, and the BBC play *Mimosa Boys* was the result. He is the author of *In Sights: The Story of a Welsh Guardsman.*

It is ordinary men who answer the call. In the field of battle, those ordinary men stand up and are forged into great men. Many of these great men pay the ultimate price. Their only reward is our freedom. It is our duty to honour their memory with love for each other.

REID, John, Lord Reid of Cardowan

Former Secretary of State for Northern Ireland
2010	*Created a Life Peer*
2006–2007	*Home Secretary*
2005–2006	*Secretary of State for Defence*
2003–2005	*Secretary of State for Health*
2003	*Leader of House of Commons*
2001–2002	*Secretary of State for Northern Ireland*
1999	*Secretary of State for Scotland*
1998–1999	*Minister for Transport*
1987–2010	*Member of Parliament*
1972	*Member of the Young Communist League*

'Man's inhumanity to man, makes countless thousands mourn.
Robert Burns, (from Man was made to mourn: A Dirge')

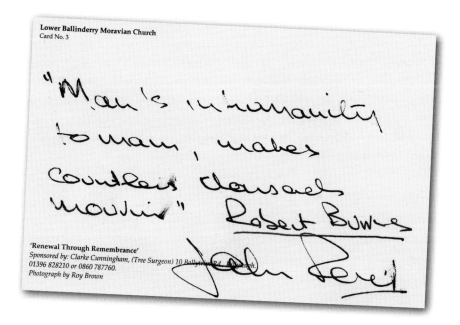

Lower Ballinderry Moravian Church
Card No. 3

"Man's inhumanity to man, makes countless thousands mournin'" Robert Burns

'Renewal Through Remembrance'
Sponsored by: Clarke Cunningham, (Tree Surgeon) 10 Ballyrogan Rd, Dromore.
01396 828210 or 0860 787760.
Photograph by Roy Brown

RIDLEY, Matthew,
KG GCVO TD, 4th Viscount Ridley

1984–2000	*Lord Lieutenant, Newcastle upon Tyne*
1988–1999	*Chancellor of Newcastle University*
1979	*Honorary Colonel of the Northumberland Hussars*
1967–1979	*Chairman of Northumberland County Council*
1964	*Succeeded his father as 4th Viscount*
1944–1945	*Served as an Officer in Normandy and Germany with the Coldstream Guards*

Later joined the Territorial Army and reached the rank of Brevet Colonel of the Northumberland Hussars

'The 4th Viscount Ridley, who has died aged 86 [on 22 March 2012] exemplified the best in conservative paternalist tradition; a businessman, naturalist and conservationist, sportsman, Knight of the Garter and courtier, he was Lord Steward of the Royal Household from 1989 to 2001.' (*Daily Telegraph*)

'It was three weeks after D-Day, and just before my 19th birthday, and I was due to fly to join my Regiment, the Coldstream Guards as a Second Lieutenant. There were 30 of us and we were due to fly from Southampton to Bayeux and none of us had ever flown before. The plane had no seats, no seat belts, no toilet and we had to sit on the filthy floor. After about one hour, one of the soldiers looked out of the window and shouted, "Look, there's France." We all jumped up and rushed to the left and we all ended up on the floor. The pilot emerged from the cockpit and screamed at us, "Get back to your places you bloody fools!" The plane had nearly crashed and he was angry.'

Rippon, Angela MBE

Journalist,
Newsreader, TV and radio presenter
Author

Angela Rippon was born in 1944 and first saw her father, who was a Royal Marine, when he returned from the Second World War in 1947.

'Memory is a wise teacher. Sadly too few pupils listen to or learn from its lessons. If they did, we might have avoided many of the bitter international and inter-community conflicts that have blighted the 20th and 21st centuries. I believe the lesson – the message – is clear: replace aggression with dialogue, compromise, compassion, understanding, and that vital quality, humanity. The world would be a more stable, settled and safer place for us all.'

MARYANG-SAN, KOREA, 4 NOVEMBER 1951

On 8 July 1951, armistice talks had opened between the belligerents in the Korean War. However, peace talks broke down in August. To combat communist intransigence, on 8 September UN Forces crossed the Imjin River to cut off the enemy salient formed by the course of the river. In early October, Operation Commando pushed deep into the salient and captured Kowang-San and to the North, Maryang-Sang. On November 4, the Chinese attacked the two summits and recaptured them. The armistice agreement was not finally signed at Panmunjom until 27 July 1953. No peace treaty has ever been signed.

Excerpt from the citation for the Victoria Cross for gallant and distinguished service in Korea, issued by the War Office, 28 December 1951:

'William Speakman V.C.
Private, 1st Battalion, The Black Watch (Royal Highlanders)
Attached 1st Btn The King's Own Scottish Borderers,
27th Commonwealth Brigade, 1st Commonwealth Division.

'From 04.00hrs, 4th November 1951, the defensive positions held by the 1st Btn, the King's Own Scottish Borderers were continuously subjected to heavy and accurate enemy shell and mortar fire.
'By 17.45hrs, fierce hand-to-hand fighting was taking place on every position.
'Private Speakman, a member of B Company, learning that the section was being overrun, decided on his own initiative to drive the enemy off the position and keep them off it. He gathered a large pile of grenades and a party of six men. Then, displaying complete disregard for his own safety, he led his party in a series of grenade attacks against the enemy.
'Having led some ten charges, through withering enemy machine gun and mortar fire, he was eventually wounded in the leg. Undaunted by his wounds, he continued to lead charge after charge against the enemy. After receiving a direct order from his superior to have his wound attended to and bandaged he immediately rejoined his comrades and led them again and again up to the time of the withdrawal of his company at 21.00hrs.

'At the critical moment of withdrawal, he assailed the enemy with showers of grenades and kept them at bay long enough for his company to effect its withdrawal.

'Under the stress and strain of this battle, Private Speakman's outstanding powers of leadership were revealed and he so dominated the situation that he inspired his colleagues to stand firm and fight the enemy to a standstill. Speakman's heroism under intense fire throughout the operation and when painfully wounded was beyond praise and is deserving of supreme recognition.'

(Supplement to *The London Gazette* of 25 December 1951, Number 39148 p.6731)

Sisters Remember

Monica Dawson, sister of the author:

'In 1966 just before his eighteenth birthday my brother was sent to fight a war in Aden. I was thirteen at the time and when the news was on we had to be quiet and Dad was serious. Mam was often in tears. On Sunday we had to listen to *Two Way Family Favourite* in case the Regiment was mentioned. It was a confusing time for us, we were a large family and none of us had ever been out of the County. We did not know what he was thinking.'

Elizabeth Dalton, sister of the author:

'I was nine years old when my brother was serving in Aden and I used to go to school and tell my teacher about him guarding the schoolchildren on the bus. He was in a band and I often thought "why can't the Bandmaster stop the fighting?" I now realise that talks fail; there are too many disagreements and I feel that wars are inevitable.'

Tebbitt, Lord, CH PC

1985–1987	*Chairman of the Conservative Party*
1985–1987	*Chancellor of the Duchy of Lancaster*
1983–1985	*Secretary of State for Trade and Industry*
1981–1983	*Secretary of State for Employment*
1970–1992	*Member of Parliament*

As a national serviceman, Norman Tebbitt flew Meteor and Vampire Jets and once had to break open the cockpit canopy of a burning Mosquito to escape.

In 1984, he was injured in the IRA bombing of the Grand Hotel in Brighton, where he was staying during the Conservative Party Conference. His wife, Margaret, was left permanently disabled by the blast. He left the government after the 1987 General Election to care for his wife.

'Terrorists can be let out of jail – none the worse for the loss of liberty for a few years, but for the victims the slate is never wiped clean. Early release has no meaning for the victim, unless it is an early release into the grave from a ruined life – or for a body broken by the barbarous use of the bodies of the innocent to gain what the terrorists wants. The bereaved grieve in their thousands, at first through every waking hour, but then as time goes past the pain comes only in sharp jabs from time to time. "How I wish he had been there to see his daughter married." Or, as the others go home to husband, wife, son or daughter, the victims go home to a house in darkness. "How I wish he were still here" – they say.

'For myself, most days I do not think about my own scars, or the bits of plastic, which hold me together. And the aches and pains when they come are what we share in old age. But every morning as I wake my wife is there beside me, still the same person she was when we were married almost fifty years ago. But no more can she sit up and say – It's a lovely day – let's go for a walk – as we did – across the moors with the children and dogs.

'For her, pain's the ever-constant companion, disability the load she never ceases to bear. For her, that quick shower and breakfast is a three-hour routine with a carer. Not for her the wheelchair-bound, the quick decision to take the train. Nor the cheap flight to Paris or Rome. No more the shared laughter at the awkward stairs – or the pokey bathroom at the village B&B

in the heart of rural France, and the fun of being off the beaten track. Never will we take those adventure trips from the brochures falling through the post box every day.

'I know how it hurts my wife that she never held her grandchildren on her knee – or prepared the treats they loved. Hers is a life of dependency. Having to ask for everything from waking to the end of her day, depending on me and the succession of carers with whom we have to share our lives. Of course there are many worse off than us by far. For many others illness or accident leaves life each day but a shadow of what might have been. But for the terrorists' victims there is the knowledge that their lives were not wrecked by illness, accident, or personal grudge, but because someone used their lives – their bodies – to bludgeon and blackmail a government to submit to their political demands.

'We, the victims, should not have to endure the sight of terrorists rewarded, nor fanatics left free to urge their followers to kill their way to paradise.

'That is just too much to bear.'

THEOBALD, Peter and Frances

Founders of the Living Memorial

This is a short extract from a letter received from Peter Theobald, who with his wife, Fran, decided to create a memorial to servicemen killed in different conflicts, with plaques listing the names and conflict zones.

'After having read of a soldier killed in 2003 in Iraq in which his wife said that before he went away he planted a lot of daffodil bulbs and now when they are growing and finally blooming she finds that it is a lasting memory to him, my conscience was pricked and several years later we decided to use some of our land to re-create this for other families and for many other conflicts.

'We put up fences, planted trees, bulbs, seats were placed so people could come and enjoy the views and peacefulness. We researched and had plaques erected to commemorate different conflict zones and the names of service people killed in them, this was originally for Iraq and Afghanistan, but as more people visited, more locations were listed and we have tried to include them.

'We named this whole project "Operation Sweat Pea", the aim being to add the names of every service personnel killed in the last 50 – 60 years to our Living Memorial.

'Our gift for the fallen troops is to leave a lasting legacy, not to glorify war, but to recognise the loss of these outstanding men and women who are undoubtedly the best of the best.'

The couple were harassed and hindered by the local council with regard to planning permission at every step of the way. Mrs Theobald says that they were dealing mainly with young people from the planning department who thought that 'Gallipoli is a meal that you order at an Italian Restaurant'.

Their project site is at:

Whitehouse Farm
Main Road
Rettendon
Chelmsford
Essex
CM3 8DL

If you would like to visit or contact them, you are very welcome.

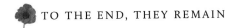
TURNER, John

Former Gunner 57, Bhurtpore Battery, 32 Heavy Regiment Royal Artillery, 1986
Former civil servant, House of Lords
Local Government Officer

Everybody Wants to Be the Hero
(But Nobody Wants to Die)

As a child you watched the war films
People died, but the hero always came home
Everybody wants to be the Hero
But nobody wants to play dead

You played 'war' in the street
If you were unlucky, somebody shouted 'You're Dead'
Everybody wants to be the hero
But nobody wants to play dead

Within five minutes you're back alive
Shooting all the baddies
Capturing the enemy castle
YOU ARE THE HERO
Everybody wants to be the hero
But nobody wants to play dead

You take those childhood ideals
You join the army
Yes, you know the risks
But it's never going to be you
Everybody wants to be a hero
But nobody wants to play dead

Unfortunately war has not seen the same films
Or played the same games
Dead is Dead
There is no coming back

EVERYBODY WANTS TO BE THE HERO
BUT NOBODY WANTS TO PLAY DEAD.

John Turner

WELLWOOD, Thomas, 'Tom'

'In 1943 I was a 15-year-old living in Newcastle and too young to join the army but I was sent, along with a bunch of retired miners, to Sunderland. Sunderland had been badly hit and there were windows to be boarded up, tarpaulin to be put on houses that had been badly damaged. Over 46,000 homes were either destroyed or badly damaged. We travelled on the back of an open-topped lorry in all types of weather. By the end of 1942 Sunderland was seeing less bombing and we were no longer needed. The people of the town were grateful for the help we had given them and, finally, in 1946, at the age of 18 I was able to enlist and was sent to Egypt for two years.'

As a North Easterner myself it must be one of the few occasions when someone from Newcastle helped someone in Sunderland! Or that they actually left Sunderland alive. (Only joking.)

WATT, General Sir Charles Redmond 'Reddy'

1998 – 2000	*General Officer Commanding the 1st (UK) Armoured Division.*
2000 – 2003	*General Officer Commanding London District*
2003 – 2005	*Commander Field Army*
2005 – 2006	*General Officer Commanding the British Army in Northern Ireland*
2007 – 2008	*Commander-in-Chief, Land Command*
2011	*Governor, the Royal Hospital Chelsea*
2011	*President of the charity, Combat Stress.*

Signed on 11th November 2005 in the hope that a more peaceful settlement and environment can be delivered in Northern Ireland with an end to Sectarianism.

WILLS, Brigadier David

Former President of the Royal British Legion
Author
Charity Director

The Royal British Legion is a leading charity providing financial, social and emotional support to those who have served and those who are serving in Her Majesty's Forces; whether on active duty or not, this support is also available to their dependents. Patron: Her Majesty Queen Elizabeth II.

> War is the manifestation of man's political poverty, greed, folly and pride; but in its darkness our path to peace is illuminated by courage, sacrifice and the ability to forgive.

WIDDECOMBE, Ann Noreen, DSG

MP 1987–2010
Former Shadow Secretary of State for Health and Shadow Home Secretary
Minister of State for Prisons
Novelist, newspaper columnist
TV celebrity

In 1990, when the PIRA murdered politician Ian Gow his seat was won by the Liberal Democrats. Upon the announcement Ann told voters that the IRA would be 'toasting their success'. Ann has been described as a social conservative and is a member of the Conservative Christian Fellowship.

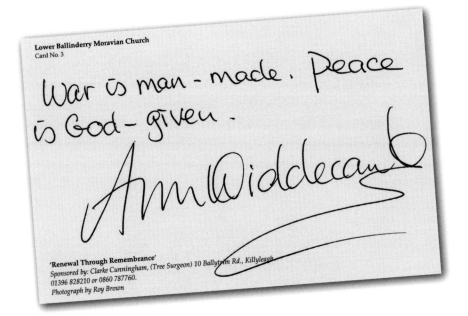

WILLIAMS, Shirley, VTB,
Baroness Williams of Crosby

Labour MP 1964–1981
SDP MP 1981–1988
Liberal Democrat MP 1988

Shirley Williams has been a fixture in British politics for decades but a less well known part of her CV is that she was a full professor at Harvard, remaining in the post until 2001, and thereafter as Public Service Professor of Electoral Politics, Emerita. She helped draft constitutions in Russia, Ukraine and South Africa. She also served as director of Harvard's 'Project Liberty', an initiative designed to assist the emerging democracies in Central and Eastern Europe.

> We each have our own heroes – my uncle, whom
> I never knew, killed in Italy in World War I; my
> brother, invalided in Egypt after World War II; and
> the thousands of others that other people loved.

Wife of a TA Soldier

Mobilisation 2004 – OPTELIC 4

'Whilst it was expected that he would be mobilised it still came as a shock. We had been trying for a baby with the knowledge that I may not be able to conceive and we found out on the 5th of January that I was expecting. My husband phoned the pay office in Glasgow who confirmed that he was on the list of those from his Territorial Regiment to be compulsory mobilised. The next few weeks were spent getting things in order, knowing and having access to all the bank accounts etc. This was a distraction and I was proud my husband was prepared to go, however I focused on the baby as the future more than anything else. On the day he left I went with him to the TA Centre. Saying goodbye was one of the hardest things I have ever done knowing that I was carrying his child. My mother gave me a poem that had provided her with comfort when my father was away during his time in the army, particularly his tour in Northern Ireland.'

The Soldier

Loving a soldier is not always gay
For with it comes a price you may have to pay
It's mostly loving with nothing to hold,
It's being young but feeling old.

It's sending a letter with a crocked stamp
A faraway love in a faraway camp
Being in love with merely a dream
Brings thoughts of heaven where lights gleam

You wish it were possible for him to phone
You wish he could call and say "I'm coming home"
And when he comes you laugh together
Unconscious of people, time or weather.

Losing a soldier is bitterness and tears
It's loneliness, sadness and unfound fears,

Reluctantly, painfully letting him go,
When your heart is crying,
Wanting him so.

We wait for the news, no more for a spell
You worry and hope that he is well
And when he comes home,
You shine with joy,
Like a small child with a brand new toy.

The contribution and sacrifices of the Territorial Army should not be under-estimated: they aren't by the regular army professionals.

'Ted Chapman left school at the age of 14 and went to work in the local colliery. He joined up in 1940 aged twenty and in 1944 he landed with his regiment in Normandy, three weeks after D-Day and served with them across France to the borders of Germany. On 2 April 1945 his unit, the Monmouthshire Regiment, was ordered to assault the Teutonburger Wald ridge ... As the Monmouths advanced, the enemy opened fire at short range inflicting heavy casualties. Grabbing a machine gun, Chapman attacked alone, firing from the hip. In reply the enemy made a determined bayonet charge. Chapman stood his ground and with his weapon halted each assault. Running out of ammunition, he called for more. The enemy ran at him hurling grenades, but he again drove them back, causing many casualties. Chapman then went out alone under fire and carried his severely wounded commander over his shoulder for fifty yards until he reached safety. On the way, both the officer and Chapman were hit, the officer fatally. In spite of a severe wound in his thigh Chapman refused all help until the position was restored two hours later. For his outstanding bravery in the face of the enemy, Chapman was awarded the Victoria Cross. After the war, he worked as a porter at Pontlottyn railway station ... He was married with three children. He died on 3 February 2002.

He was a Territorial soldier.'

Obituary, (London) *Independent*, 5 February 2002

WHARTON, Ken

'I was very honoured and flattered when Raymond Clark asked me to write a few short words for his new book and my first reaction was to wonder what a soldier-scribe, as I was once described, could contribute. I joined the British Army at 17 and although my military service was neither over-long nor particularly distinguished, my love for my Regiment and my admiration for the wider Army has grown exponentially over the years. I will support the "squaddie" in his attempts to win peace, to defend his country and to fight the wars which the politicians start. I have my own intimate experience of Northern Ireland to draw upon and I have also witnessed from afar our magnificent efforts in the South Atlantic, in the hate-filled villages of Bosnia, in the deserts of Kuwait and Iraq, and the mountainous and violent regions of Afghanistan. Wherever he fights, the British soldier does so with honour, with professionalism and with compassion for his fellow man and I would venture to claim that we have treated our defeated enemies with kindness and humanity.

'In Northern Ireland, we fought on our own doorstep, in our "own back yard" so to speak and in the face of incredible and increasing hatred as we struggled to bring law and order to that beleaguered part of the United Kingdom. Had we been soldiers in a tin pot military junta in South America, SS troops in the last war or even Americans in Vietnam, we would have left behind piles of bullet-riddled corpses on every street corner of Belfast, Londonderry, Newry and Crossmaglen. We kept the peace with an almost sanguine optimism and a belief in ourselves as both soldiers and as humanitarians. That we didn't resort to revenge killings and indiscriminate atrocities is indeed tribute to our restraint and professionalism and one cannot imagine any other army of any other nation which would have acted in the same way as the British soldier did in Northern Ireland.

'The soldier of any nationality, be he British, Australian, American, Russian or Japanese, does the bidding of his political masters. The men – and women – in suits, sit in privileged positions and use the lives of their soldiers as pawns in a huge game of international politics. The politician "makes" the bullets for our soldiers to fire and the soldier does this uncomplainingly and he does it well and he does it professionally. He expects to die and it is a bonus when he can return to his loved ones. His loved ones, in return, expect that he be well rewarded for his service and should the worst happen, that those politicians who sent their husband or son off to fight "their" war will remember that service and pay a moral debt to those left behind.

'One is reminded of the Falklands commemoration where the badly wounded and maimed survivors were made to sit at the back of Westminster Abbey so as not to cause offence. To borrow from Neil Kinnock, all politicians have "guts" and it is a great pity that others have to lay theirs down at places such as Goose Green, Basra and Warrenpoint to prove it.

'The great Rudyard Kipling wrote a superb poem about the British soldier that includes the lines *"For it's Tommy this, an' Tommy that, an 'Chuck him out, the brute!' But it's 'Saviour of 'is country,' when the guns begin to shoot."* Those words, penned in 1882, are still true today, over 120 years later. It makes my blood boil that "Muslims Against Crusades" should be allowed to protest at soldiers' homecoming parades and scream offensive abuse as the returning soldiers, several of their numbers short, march through their towns. It sickens me when I read of local residents in the Midlands who are objecting to the turning of an old building into a convalescent centre for wounded veterans. It reduces me to an absolute rage when I hear that women in some areas have objected to local swimming baths cordoning off several lanes for maimed soldiers to be given water therapy. Finally, I shed tears of impotent fury when I read of a dreadfully wounded soldier being insulted in a fish n' chip shop in the south of England. Kipling was so right and I feel utter contempt for the people who have shamed my country through their insensitivity and their insults.

'I am proud to have been a British soldier, proud to have been a member of the finest army in the world and I am honoured to write these words for Raymond's book.'

DO NOT STAND AT MY GRAVE AND WEEP

On the 9 March 1989 a family were given the sad news that their son had been killed in Londonderry, Northern Ireland, when the Land Rover he was travelling in was blown up as it went over a landmine. In the possession of the family at the time was a letter that the son had written before he went to Northern Ireland, which was to be opened in the event of his death. With this letter was a poem:

> Do not stand at my grave and weep
> I am not there, I do not sleep
> I am a thousand winds that blow
> I am the diamond glint in the snow
>
> I am the sunlight on ripened grain
> I am the gentle autumn rain.
> When you awake in the morning's rush
> I am the swift uplifting rush
> Of quiet birds in circled flight
>
> I am the soft stars that shine at night.
> Do not stand at my grave and cry
> I am not there – I did not die.

The poem was almost certainly written by Mary Elizabeth Frye of Baltimore in 1932. This poem appeared the following day in the *Daily Mail* and was also read out on TV; the young man's father then read it out on Remembrance Sunday that same year. Since then a CD has been made, and the poem has been used at many funerals and remembrance services around the world. It was used at a commemorative service for the astronauts of the ill-fated Challenger Space Shuttle.

THE SOLDIER

Words and music by Harvey Andrews, singer, song-writer and musician, reproduced by kind permission of Harvey Andrews and Westminster Music Ltd.

In a station in the city a British soldier stood
Talking to the people if the people would
Some just stared in hatred, and others turned in pain
And the lonely British Soldier wished he was back home again.

Come join the British Army! Said the posters in the town
See the world and have your fun and serve before the crown
The jobs were hard to come by and he could not face the dole
So he took his country's shilling and enlisted on the roll.

For there was no fear of fighting, the Empire long was lost
Just ten years in the army getting paid for being bossed
The leave a man experienced, a man who's made the grade
A medal, a pension, some mem'ries and a trade.

Then came the call to Ireland as the call had come before
Another bloody chapter in an endless civil war
The priests they stood on both sides, the priests stood behind
Another fight in Jesus' name, the blind against the blind.

The soldier stood between them, between the whistling stones
And then the broken bottles that led to broken bones
The petrol bombs that burnt his hands, the nails that pierced his skin
And wished he'd stayed at home surrounded by his kin.

The station filled with people, the soldier soon was bored
But better in the station than where the people warred
The rooms filled up with mothers and daughters and with sons
Who stared with itchy fingers at the soldier and his gun.

A yell of fear, the screech of brakes, the shattering of glass
The window of the station broke to let the package pass
A scream came from the mothers as they ran towards the door
Dragging their children crying from the bomb upon the floor.

The soldier stood and could not move. His gun he could not use
He knew the bomb had seconds and not minutes on the fuse
He could not run to pick it up and throw it in the street
There were far too many people there, too many running feet.

Take cover! yelled the soldier. Take cover for your lives
And the Irishmen threw down their young and stood before their wives
They turned towards the soldier their eyes alive with fear
For God's sake save our children or they'll end their young lives here.

The soldier moved towards the bomb his stomach like a stone
Why was this his battle God, why was he alone?
He lay down on the package and he murmured one farewell
To those at home in England to those he loved so well.

He saw the sights of summer, felt the wind upon his brow
The young girls in the city parks how precious were they now
The soaring of the swallow, the beauty of the swan
The music of the turning world would soon be gone.

A muffled soft explosion and the room began to quake
The soldier blown across the floor, his blood a crimson lake
There was no time to cry or shout there was no time to moan
And they turned children's faces from the blood and from the bones.

The crowd outside soon gathered and the ambulances came
To carry off the body of a pawn lost in the game
And the crowd they clapped and cheered as they sang their rebel song
One soldier less to interfere where he did not belong.

And will the children growing up learn at their mothers' knee
The story of the soldier who bought their liberty
Who used his youthful body as a means towards the end
Who gave his life to those who call him murderer not friend.

THE GOOD FRIDAY AGREEMENT

The document was sent to every household in Northern Ireland and The Republic of Ireland. I sent copies to every politician who had put his or her signature to the original document. They were asked if they would sign. The signed copy was sold for charity.

At first, some signatories would not oblige until the personal intervention of Senator George Mitchell after he spoke to me from Washington. He told me not to worry; the job would be completed and forwarded to me with his best wishes. Thank you Senator.

The signatories:

Tony Blair, Prime Minister of the UK; Bill Clinton, President of the United States; Bertie Ahern, Taisoch of the Republic of Ireland; Marjorie 'Mo' Mowlam, Secretary of State for Northern Ireland; John Hulme, Leader of the SDLP; David Trimble, Leader of the UUP; David Ervine, Leader of the PUP; Jerry Adams, Leader of Sinn Fein; George Mitchell, United States Senator.

WAR MEMORIALS

What does a war memorial mean and signify to you? Does it mean that we are celebrating war? Does it mean that we are glorifying war? I do not know and cannot tell what it means to you, but I do know what it means to me. To me it is a permanent monument to those who have died or been killed as a result of working for their country under a stress and strain that we, in our ordinary day-to-day lives, know nothing about. They died as both volunteers and as conscripted individuals.

It is visual in that we can see it; it is made of stone, concrete, marble, wood and metal. It can be a wall, a statue, a plaque, a cross or a large structure such as the Cenotaph in London. It is also verbal, or vocal, because as we look at the names carved with pride, each name speaks out to us and calls us to remember that they were grandfathers, fathers, husbands, uncles, nephews and sometimes mothers, daughters. Each had their own problems, their insecurities and their own lives. They suffered pain, or if they were 'lucky', they were killed instantly.

Amongst those names are people who would never have their own families, careers or grandchildren. They were people who once thought like you and I. They thought, 'I will grow up and do all those things that my parents tell me not to do. I will meet someone, fall in love, marry and have a job and family, and then, in old age, I will reminisce.'

As you stand at Remembrance Day Parade or attend a service in an unheated church in your hat, gloves and coat with the thought of a nice cuppa afterwards, will you stop to think about the cold, damp, hunger and fear that those names you are honouring felt? Amongst those lost may have been that special someone who would come up with some great medical breakthrough, they might have been a prime minister, an artist – you will never know.

Think about those names as real people the next time you look at a memorial, and the next time you see an old codger proudly wearing his medals, let your eyes and mind go past the outer shell and look at his soul and imagine the pain that he possibly feels knowing that he survived and they did not. He once was young with ambitions. Now he is old. But he is still a person with memories of when he and his pals were, like you, alive and young.

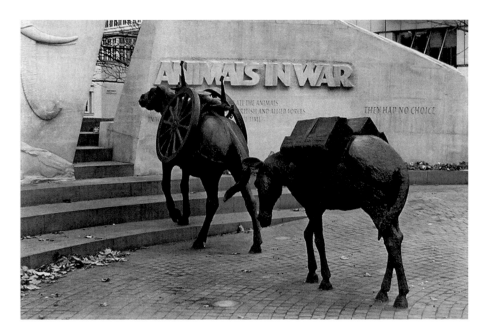

We all need to awake our consciousness to enable us to play our part to ensure that no more names are added.

That there are no more wars or conflicts.

That there is no more needless loss of life.

That there are no more tears shed.

That there are no more lives ruined and more memorials are not needed.

Remember to stop seeing an old man and see the young person that was.

MEDALS

The Victoria Cross – The highest military award for gallantry. Seven holders are pictured below in 1898. Five had been defenders at Rorke's Drift. Private Bell (seated, far left) had won his VC for a sea rescue in the Andaman Islands, Lt Col E.S. Browne (seated, centre left) won his during the Zulu campaign at Inhlobani Hill.

The George Cross – Second only to the Victoria Cross, this is the highest civilian award for gallantry. The George Cross can be made to military personnel for acts of heroism not in the face of the enemy.

The Military Cross – The Military Cross is granted in recognition of 'an act or acts of exemplary gallantry during active operations against the enemy on land to all members of any rank in our Armed Forces.' In 1979, the Queen approved a proposal that a number of awards, including the Military Cross, could be awarded posthumously.

The Elizabeth Cross – This was instituted by Queen Elizabeth II on 1 July 2009. It is awarded to the next of kin of servicemen and women who died during operations or were killed as a result of terrorist action since the Second World War. It is made of hallmarked silver carrying the Rose of England, the Scottish thistle, the Irish shamrock and the Welsh daffodil. The cross is backed by a representation of a laurel wreath. Families receive a large version the cross and a pin-on miniature, together with a Memorial Scroll signed by the Queen, which bears the name of the person who died.

SOME THOUGHTS ON THE UNIQUE FORMER BRITISH REGIMENTAL SYSTEM

'Staff Officers might speak of general actions if they would, but, except to such inferior mortals, a battle was purely a regimental matter and must be treated as such. And hence it was that when one man in every two, or even two in every three, had fallen in Hoghton's brigade the survivors were still in line by their colours, closing in towards the tattered silk which represented the ark of their covenant, the one thing supremely important to them in the world.'
Sir John Fortescue

'Regiments are not like houses, they cannot be pulled down and altered structurally to suit the convenience of the occupier or the caprice of the owner. They are more like plants; they grow slowly if they are to grow strong ... and if they are blighted or transplanted they are apt to wither.'
Winston Churchill

'A significant fact brought to light in the Great War is, that notwithstanding units being re-duplicated over and over again, they all appeared to inherit the esprit de corps of their regiments and fully acted up to the tradition of the regiment of which they formed part.'
Charles Pelham, K.G.

AFTERWORD
BY RAYMOND CLARK

These are my own personal thoughts and beliefs. Our servicemen and women are and will be sent to fight and perhaps die to ensure that not only the people of this land but also the peoples of other nations are able to live in freedom. Freedom to exercise the right of free speech. Freedom to experience life without fear and oppression from the state. Freedom to live without wars. They fight and die for the human rights accorded to each and every one of us. The human rights of *all*.

Human rights are the rights to which we are all entitled as individuals; they are for all and not just minority groups. Such groups wish to preserve their rights by disallowing and ignoring those of the majority. We are unable to deport those who threaten our way of life, threaten to hurt, to maim and kill as a means towards their ends. We are unable to deport them because their human rights will be affected by the threat of inhumane treatment or death if they are deported. What about the threat to the lives of the silent majority and their human rights?

The public are tolerant, patient and understanding. They understand that our politicians, civil leaders and the legal system will not speak out for them. Why will no one speak out?

They are afraid. They are afraid of a system that they themselves created. They are afraid of 'upsetting' the minority, and it easier to upset the majority, who do not complain and are long-suffering – but for how long?

Our servicemen and women have paid, and will continue to pay, with their lives for that silence.

It's the military, not the reporter, who have given us freedom of the press.

It's the military, not the poet, who have given us freedom of speech.

It's the military, not the politicians, who give us liberty.

It's the military that salute the flag.

It's the military that serve beneath the flag.

It's the military, not the politicians, whose coffins are draped in the flag.

The Final Inspection

The soldier stood and faced God,
Which must always come to pass.
He hoped his shoes were shining,
Just as brightly as his brass.

'Step forward now, you soldier,
How shall I deal with you?
Have you always turned the other cheek?
To my church have you always been true?'

The soldier squared his shoulders and said,
'No, Lord, I guess I have not.
Because those of us who carry guns,
Can't always be a saint.

I've had to work most Sundays,
At times my talk has been tough.
Sometimes I've been violent,
Because the world is awfully rough.

But, I've never taken a penny,
That wasn't always mine to keep ...
I sometimes worked a lot of overtime,
When the bills got too steep.

And I never passed a cry for help,
Though at times I shook with fear.
And sometimes, God, forgive me,
I've wept unmanly tears.

I know I don't deserve a place,
Among the people here.
They never wanted me around,
Except to calm their fears.

If you've a place for me here, Lord,
It needn't be so grand.
I never expected or had too much,
But if you don't, I'll understand.'

There was silence all around the throne,
Where the saints had often trod.
As the soldier waited quietly,
For the judgement of his God.

'Step forward now, you soldier.
You've borne your burdens well.
Walk peacefully on Heaven's streets,
You've done your time in hell.'

I VOW TO THEE MY COUNTRY

I vow to thee, my country, all earthly things above,
Entire and whole and perfect, the service of my love:
The love that asks no question, the love that stands the test,
That lays upon the altar the dearest and the best;
The love that never falters, the love that pays the price,
The love that makes undaunted the final sacrifice.

And there's another country, I've heard of long ago,
Most dear to them that love her, most great to them that know;
We may not count her armies, we may not see her King;
Her fortress is a faithful heart, her pride is suffering;
And soul by soul and silently her shining bounds increase,
And her ways are ways of gentleness and all her paths are peace.

This hymn conjures up many things and is used for many occasions; it has been used at weddings, including both the Queen's and Princess Diana's. It is played at funerals; it was played at the funeral of my wife, Cynthia. It is synonymous with patriotism and has even been played as a 'second national anthem' at sporting events. It also speaks to, and for, the soldier.

Some denominations are reviewing hymnals and have removed it from their books because it is considered 'nationalistic' and, as such, is not 'politically correct'. Let the public decide what is correct and let politicians and cultural elites do what they do best.

SOLDIER'S SONGS

This is my list; yours will be quite different. It features a few songs that may bring back memories of conflict to former or present members of the armed forces.

I Will Carry You
(The Soldiers)

Here's to the Blokes in the Falkland Isles

A Hard Rain's a-Gonna Fall
(Bob Dylan)

The Soldier
(Harvey Andrew). The BBC banned this song.

Universal Soldier
(Donovan)

Give Peace a Chance
(John and Yoko)

Daddy's Home
(Cliff Richard)

There Won't Be Many Coming Home
(Roy Orbison). Although concerning the war in Vietnam, BFBS Radio in Aden banned it in the mid-'60s when the conflict there was at its height.

We'll Meet Again
(Vera Lynn)

Wherever You Are
(The Military Wives Choir). This record sold over 300,000 copies within three days.

RECOMMENDED READING

The Bedford Boys – One Small Town's D-Day Sacrifice. Alan Kershaw

Beyond the Legend: Bill Speakman VC. Derek Hunt and John Mulholland

The Bloodiest Year: 1972. Ken Wharton

Bullets, Bombs and Cups of Tea. Ken Wharton

Embed: With the World's Armies in Afghanistan. Nick Allen

Famous Regiments of the British Army, Vols I and II. Dorian Bond
(All royalties earned from the sales of these books are kindly donated by the author to Help for Heroes.)

Four Weeks in May – The Loss of HMS Coventry. David Hart Dyke

Marie, A Story from Enniskillen. Gordon Wilson

Rats, The Story of a Dog Soldier. Max Halstock

Shadow. Michael Morpurgo
(A children's book, but no worse for that, based on the story of Sali, a black Labrador with the Australian Special Forces in Afghanistan.)

Sister Kate, Nursing through the Troubles. Kate O'Hanlon
(Sister Kate was Casualty Sister during my time in NI, and she was a very formidable sister from the old school and reigned with the style and presence of the late Hattie Jacques. When the 'Red Sister' was on duty, the department was on its toes.)

Unscathed – Escape from Sierra Leone. Major Phil Ashby

THANK YOU

There are so many to whom I would like to say thank you for making this book possible, and they include:

Shaun Barrington (The man who said 'yes')
The History Press
All contributors
John Turner (technical advice with computer design)
Andrew Hall (for advice, encouragement and proofreading)
Henry and Anne (for being there)
Clarke Cunningham of Killyleagh, Northern Ireland, James Andrew Hall and John Turner of Bournemouth kindly sponsored the cards sold and sent out.
Thanks to Nick Allen for great pictures from his book *Embed: With the World's Armies in Afghanistan.*
Thanks to Bill Jones for the evocative illustrations.
Everyone who encouraged me in those moments of doubt, and there were a few.
My late wife, Cynthia, for getting me started.
My daughter, Jillian.

Best wishes for our efforts were been received from, amongst others:

HRH the Duchess of Cornwall
Their Royal Highnesses the Princes William and Harry
HRH The Duke of Kent
Pope Pius XVI

Clearly, it would be difficult for such public figures to express their own personal views on this subject in print.

And last but not least, I would like to thank you, for buying the book – and in so doing contributing to such good causes.

If I have missed anyone, then I really am sorry, and I owe you a pint next time we meet.